First published in Great Britain in 2001
by Collins & Brown Limited
64 Brewery Road
London N7 9NT
A member of **Chrysalis** Books plc

3 5 7 9 8 6 4 2

British Library Cataloguing-in-Publication Data:
A catalogue record for this book
is available from the British Library.

ISBN 1 85585 871 1 (paperback edition)

Conceived, edited and designed by
Collins & Brown Limited

Editor: Kate Haxell
Design: Jonathon Raimes and Kate Haxell
Illustrations: Kuo Kang Chen and Dominic Harris
Photography: Matthew Dickens

Reproduction by Global Colour
Printed and bound in Singapore by Tat Wei

Distributed in the United States and Canada by
Sterling Publishing Co, 387 Park Avenue South,
New York, NY 10016, USA

# HOW TO USE THIS BOOK

A question we are often asked, by both beginners to the art of glass painting and skilled enthusiasts, is quite simply, 'Where can I find motifs to paint?'. Until now we have had to suggest either ploughing through lots of different magazines and books or drawing your own motifs.

Now, however, we have a perfect answer to that often-asked question: this book, which is packed with over 1,000 different motifs, all especially selected for glass painting, is exactly what you need. We have put our heads together and chosen motifs that we know are popular and added more from our favourite themes. So, whether you want geometric panels, flowers, children's motifs, dragons or alphabets, this book has a selection to choose from.

The book is broken down into small, specific sections and within those sections every motif is numbered. So, not only is it easy to look up a particular motif, but it is also simple to find it again. The detailed contents list on pages 4-7 will guide you through the different sections in the book.

Each motif is a black-line artwork, ready to be outlined onto glass and painted. If the motif you have chosen is the size you want, then just trace it off in black pen and start work. If, however, you want to use the motif larger or smaller than it is given, you have two options.

Enlarging or reducing the design on a photocopier is the easiest and quickest way of getting the design to the right size. If you do not have access to a photocopier, then you can alter the size of a design by the grid method. Trace off your chosen design and, with a ruler, draw a grid over it, making the lines about 5mm (¼in) apart. On a sheet of white paper, draw another grid, with the same number of horizontal and vertical lines, but spacing the lines wider apart, so that the finished grid covers the area you want the completed design to fill. Following the traced-off design and working in one square of the grid at a time, copy that area onto the larger grid. When you have finished you will have a design of the right size ready to work from.

For those of you who are beginners to the art of glass painting, we have included a step-by-step section on the basic outlining technique, plus some helpful tips. There are also steps showing how to transfer designs onto mirrors and curved glass, so you can paint bottles and vases.

With so many designs to choose from, we hope that this book will keep you inspired for years to come.

Alan D. Gear and Barry L. Freestone

# CONTENTS

# MAKING AN OUTLINING BAG

A triangle of greaseproof paper is the basis of an outlining bag, which can be filled with outliner, paint or glue, and is easy to use. It is cost effective, as you can buy larger bottles of a product, which are often cheaper than smaller ones, and fill your bags from them. If you don't use all the contents of an outlining bag, you can squeeze them back into the bottle.

**step 1**
Cut a 20cm (8in) square of good-quality greaseproof paper and cut it in half diagonally to give you two triangles. Take one triangle and, with the centre point towards you, you curl one corner point over so that it meets the centre point and forms a cone.

**step 2**
Hold the points together at the bottom and take the other corner over the top of the cone and round to the back, making a double-skinned cone.

**step 3**
With your thumbs on the inside of the cone, push the paper downwards and inwards. At the same time, your fingers, on the outside of the bag, should push the outside flap backwards and outwards. This will make the tip of the cone very tight.

**step 4**
Hold the paper firmly and fold the points at the open end over, into the cone, twice, to stop the bag unfurling.

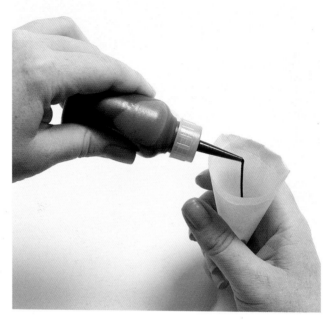

### step 5
Fill the cone halfway up with outliner. Do not over-fill it or it will be difficult to close and the contents will ooze out.

### step 6
Fold both of the corners of the bag in at an angle, as shown.

**step 7**
Now fold this end of the bag over several times to close it firmly. The bag should be fat and firm and, if you have made it properly, none of the contents will ooze out.

**step 8**
Now cut the tip of the bag off with a pair of scissors to make a hole the size you want. It is better to cut a smaller hole first: you can always enlarge it if necessary. As you use the contents, fold the end of the bag over further to keep it fat and firm.

# HOW TO OUTLINE

Always try to outline towards yourself, the outliner will flow better and you can easily see what you are doing. Work on the area of glass directly in front of you and turn the glass round as you go – don't lean over areas of wet outliner as you may smudge them. If your hand trembles, support your wrist with your other hand. Keep a piece of kitchen paper to hand to wipe any blobs off the tip of the bag and if any outliner gets on your clothes, wash it out immediately.

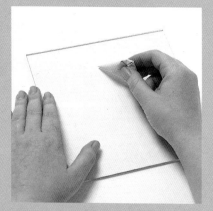

**step 1**
To begin outlining, touch the tip of the outlining bag to the glass where you want the line to start.

**step 2**
Squeeze the bag quite firmly and, as the outliner emerges from the bag, lift the tip up, away from the glass. Keep squeezing the bag so that the outliner flows at a smooth rate. Lay the line of outliner down on the glass, keeping the tip of the bag about 1cm (½in) above the surface. If your outliner breaks in mid-line, touch the tip of the bag to the broken end and continue the line.

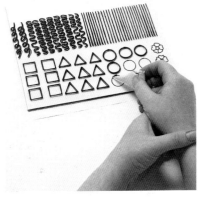

### step 3

When you want to finish the line, stop squeezing the bag and touch the tip to the glass where you want the line to stop. To finish the line neatly, lift the tip away from the glass in the direction that the line is travelling.

### step 4

To perfect your outlining technique, lay a piece of glass or plastic over the practice sheet (see page 17). Starting with the straight lines, work your way around the page many times, washing off the outliner after each completed sheet.

# MAKING OUTLINING EASIER

There are two ways to make outlining easier: use coloured templates and correct any mistakes the right way.

To make a coloured design, either have it photocopied in a different colour or trace or draw it in coloured pen (see page 3). As for correcting mistakes in outliner, we have tried many ways over the years, and this is definitely the best.

### using coloured templates

If you are using black outliner over a black-line template, you may find it difficult to see where you have outlined and where is still to be done, especially if you are using thick 6mm (¼in) glass. To make everything clearer, use a template in a different colour to the outliner you are using.

### correcting mistakes

If you make a mistake you can try to wipe it off straight away. However, we find it more precise, and less messy, to let the outliner dry, then cut the mistake out with a craft knife and re-draw the line with fresh outliner.

# TRANSFERRING A TEMPLATE ONTO CURVED GLASS

It can be tricky to accurately outline over a template onto a curved glass item but, if you want to work straight onto the glass with ordinary outliner, this is the best way of going about it.

### step 1

Using scissors, cut out the template closely, cutting in between the elements of the design as much as possible, but keeping the template in one piece. Place the template inside the glass item and, pushing it up against the glass, tape it in position with small pieces of masking tape.

### step 2

Outline the design in the usual way (see *how to outline*, page 12). If you are working on a large glass item, cushion it on a rolled-up piece of fabric or a towel. If the design is right around the item, outline it in sections, letting each section dry before you move on to the next one.

# TRANSFERRING A TEMPLATE ONTO MIRROR GLASS

Outlining onto mirror glass presents a problem, as obviously you can't see a design placed underneath it. The answer is to use carbon paper to transfer the design from paper onto the mirror glass.

**step 1**

Place the carbon paper face down on the mirror. Place the design on top, and tape it in position if necessary. Trace over the design with a pen or pencil, pressing down to imprint the lines onto the mirror. Peel off the carbon paper to reveal the transferred design.

**step 2**

Outline the design (see *how to outline*, page 12). When the outliner is dry, wipe off any remaining carbon ink with a cloth before you start painting the mirror glass, or it will discolour the paints.

1.flowers

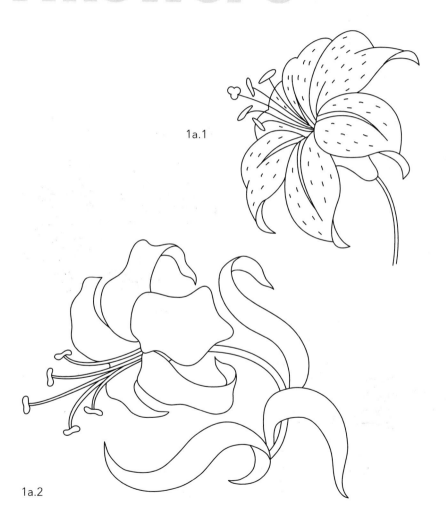

1a.1

1a.2

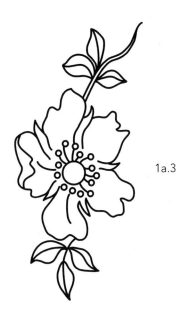

1a.3

1a.4

1a.5

1a.7

1a.6

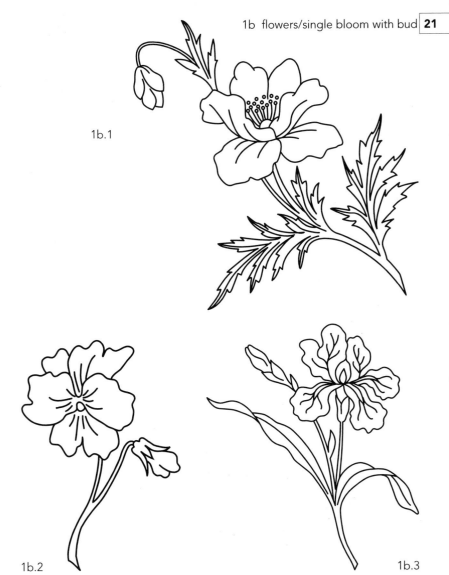

1b.1

1b.2

1b.3

1b.4

1b.5

1b.6

1b.7

1b.8

1b.9

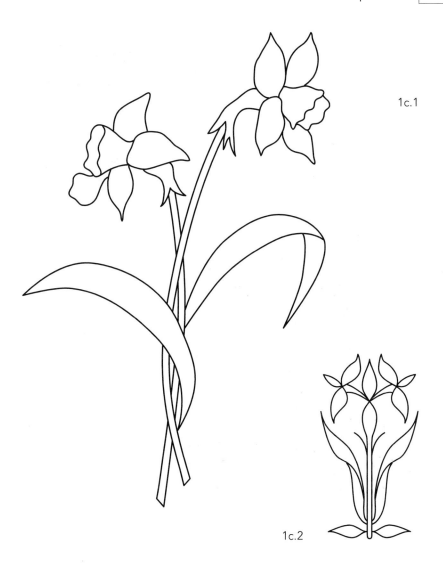

1c.1

1c.2

1c.3

1c.4

1c.5

1c.6

1c.7

1c.8

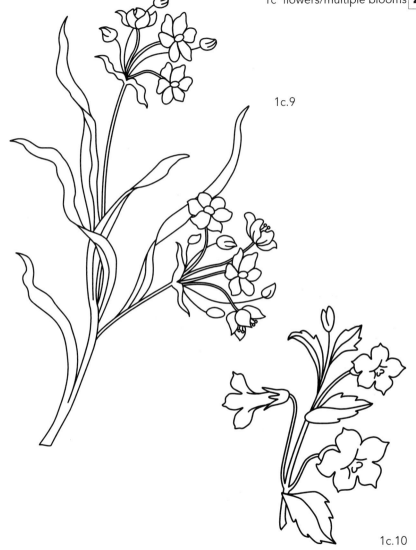

1c.9

1c.10

1c.11

1c.12

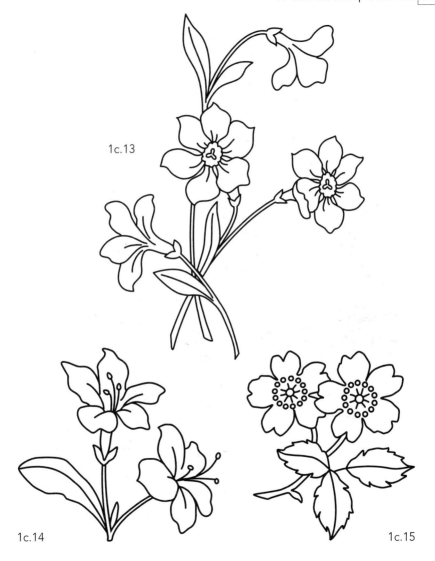

1c.13

1c.14

1c.15

1c.16

1c.17

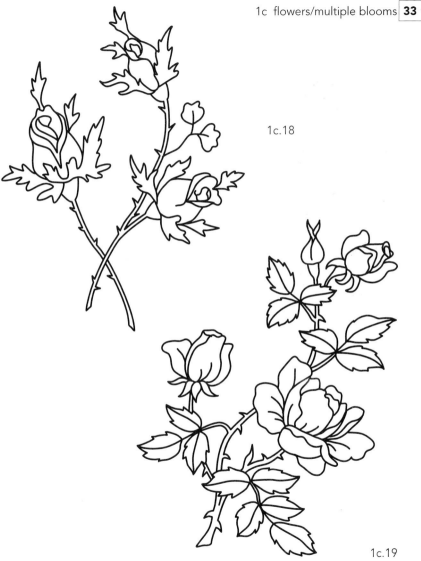

1c.18

1c.19

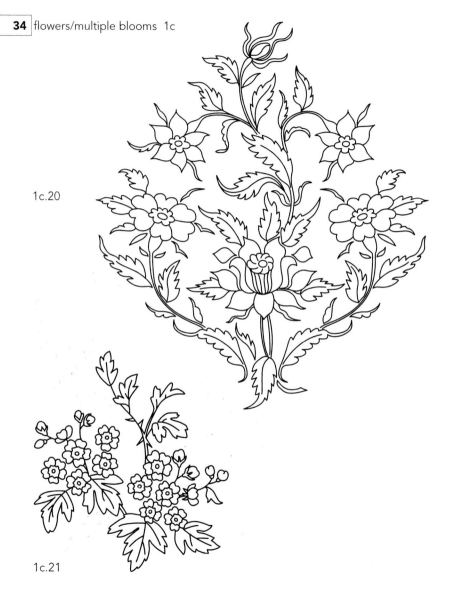

1c.20

1c.21

1c.22

1c.23

1c.24

1c.25

1c.26

1c.27

1c.28

1c.29

1c.30

1c.31

1c.33

1c.32

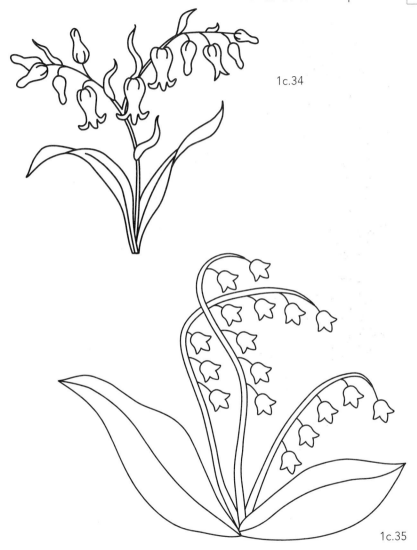

1c.34

1c.35

1c.36

1c.37

1c.38

1c.39

1c.40

1c.41

1d.1

1d.2

1d.3

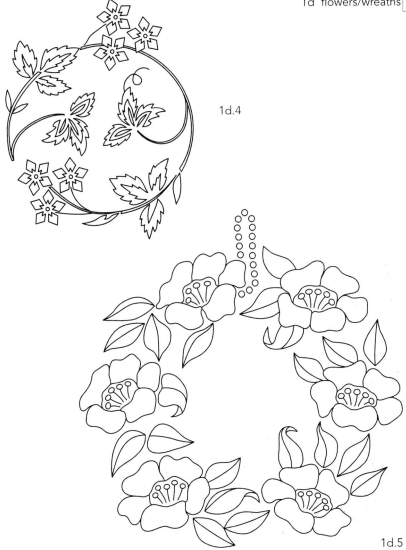

1d.4

1d.5

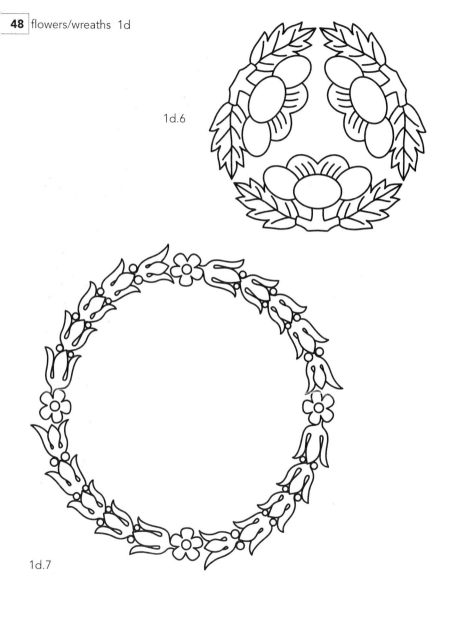

1d.6

1d.7

1e.1

1e.2

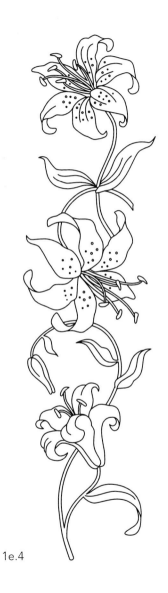

1e.3

1e.4

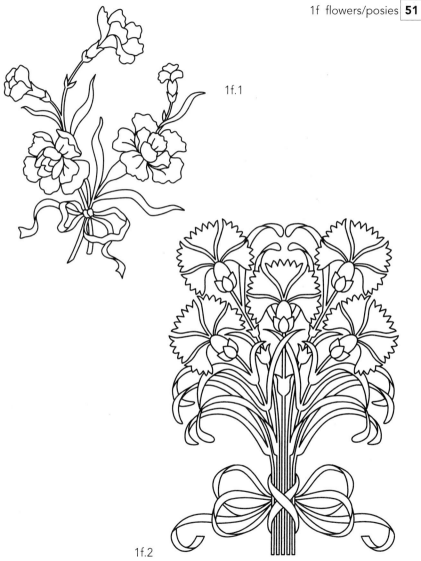

1f.1

1f.2

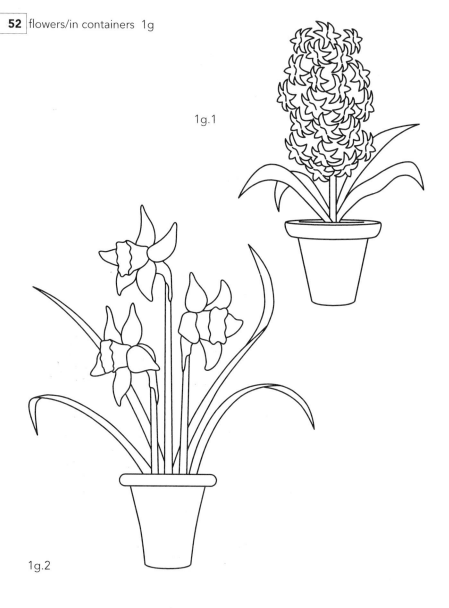

1g.1

1g.2

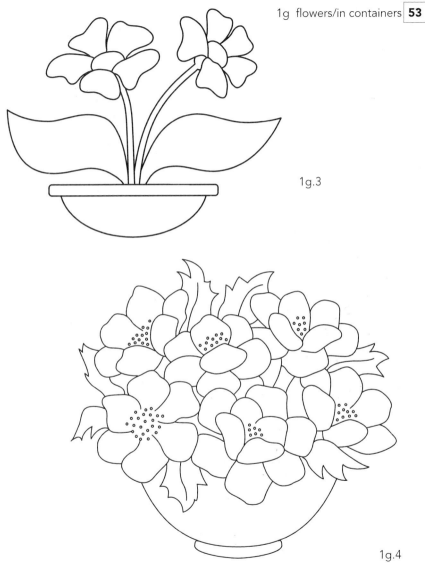

1g.3

1g.4

1g.5

1g.6

1g.7

1g.8

1g.9

1g.10

1g.11

1g.12

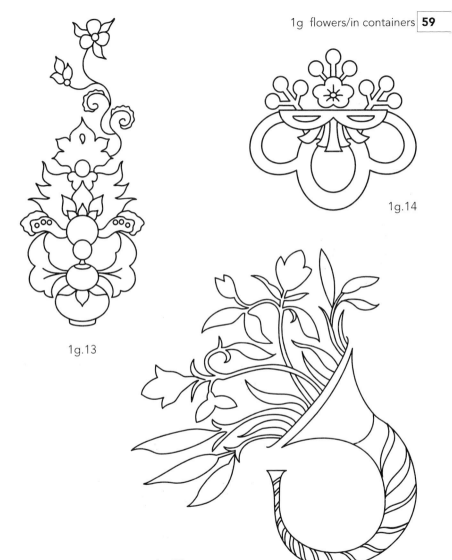

1g.14

1g.13

1g.15

1h.1

1h.2

1h.3

1h.4

1h.5

1h.6

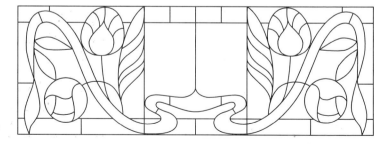

1h.7

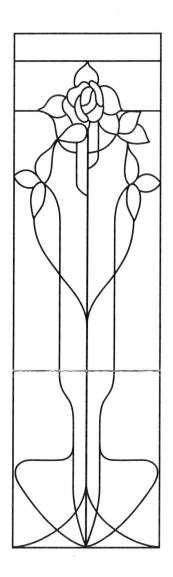

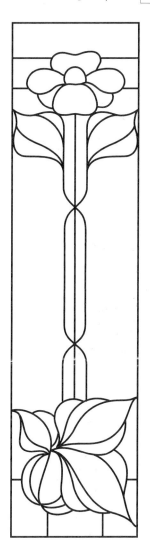

1h.8        1h.9

1h.10

1h.11

1h.12

1h.13

1h.14

1h.15

1h.16

1h.17

1h.18

1i.1

1i.2

1i.3

1i.4

1i.5

1i.6

1i.7

1i.8

1i.9

1i.10

1i.11

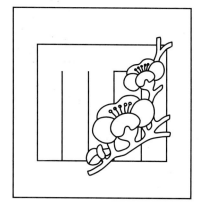

1i.12

1i.13

1j.1

1j.2

1k.1

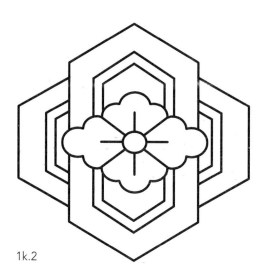

1k.2

1k.3

1k.4

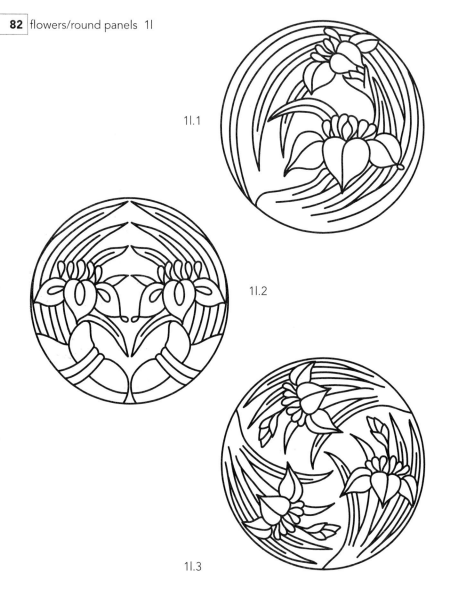

1l.1

1l.2

1l.3

1l.4

1l.5

1l.6

1l.7

1l.8

1l.9

1l.10

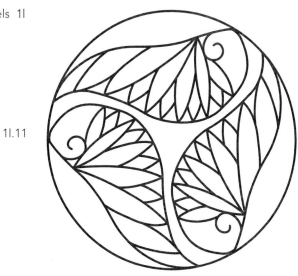

1l.11

1l.12

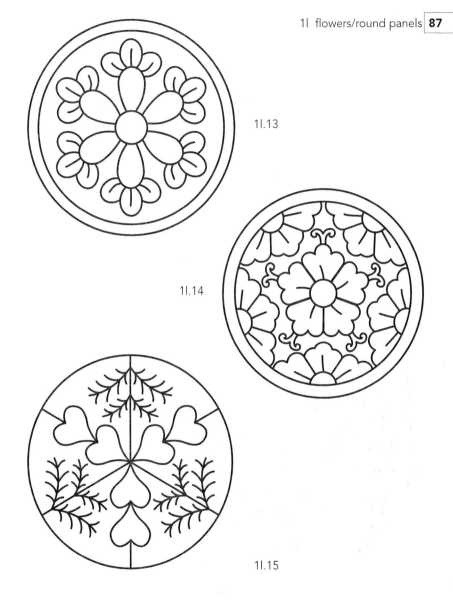

1l.13

1l.14

1l.15

1l.16

1l.17

1l.18

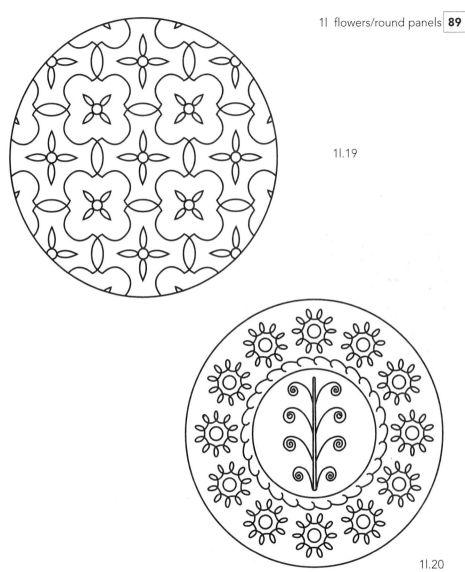

1I.19

1I.20

1l.21

1l.22

1I.23

1I.24

1m.1

1m.2

1m.3

1m.4

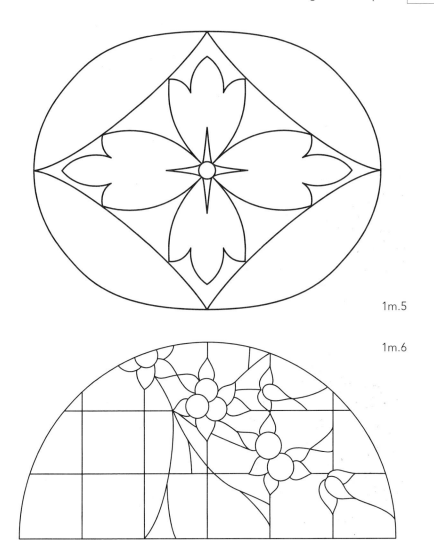

1m.5

1m.6

1n.1

1n.2

1n.3

1n.4

1n.5

1n.6

1n.7

1n.8

1n.9

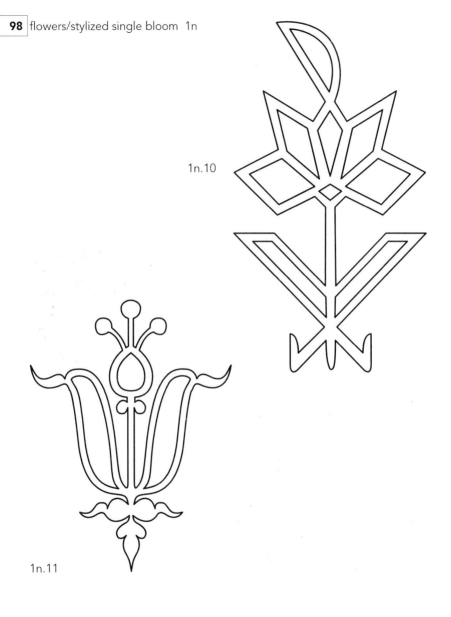

1n.10

1n.11

1n.12

1n.13

1n.14

1n.15

1n.16

1n.17

1n.18

1n.19

1n.20

1n.21

1n.22

1o.1

1o.2

1o.3

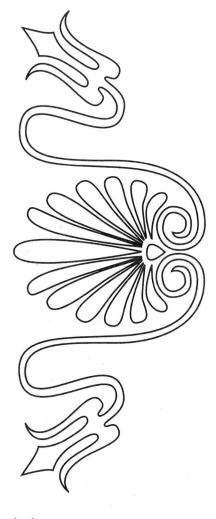

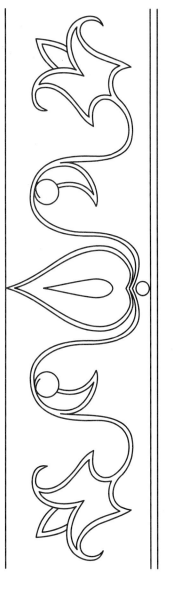

1o.4

1o.5

1o.6

1o.7

1o.8

1o.9

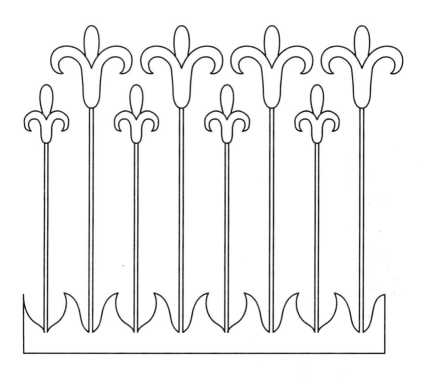

1o.10

1o.11

1o.12

1o.13

1o.14

1o.15

1o.16

1o.17

1o.18

1o.19

1o.20

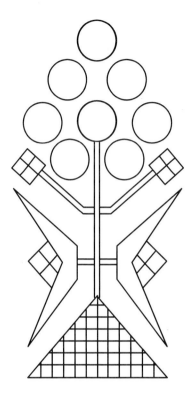

1o.21

1o.22

2a.1

2a.2

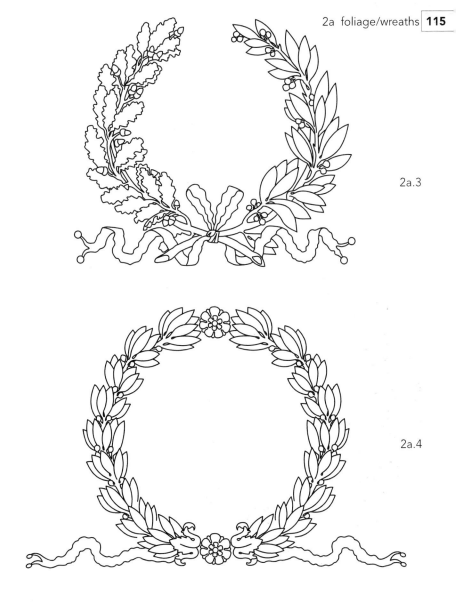

2a.3

2a.4

2a.5

2a.6

2a.7

2a.8

2a.9

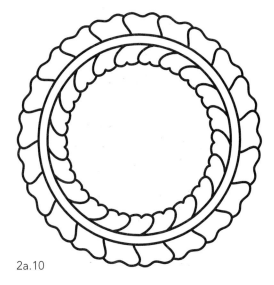

2a.10

2b.1

2b.2

2b.3

2b.4

2c.1

2c.2

2c.3

2c.4

2c.5

2d.1

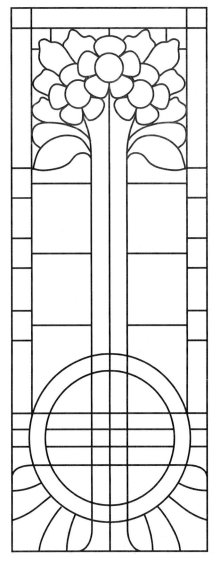

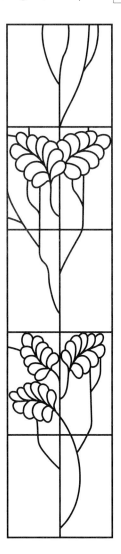

2d.2    2d.3

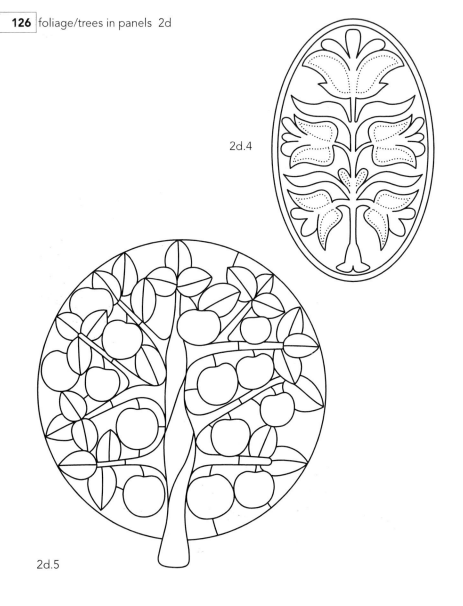

2d.4

2d.5

2e.1

2e.2

2e.3

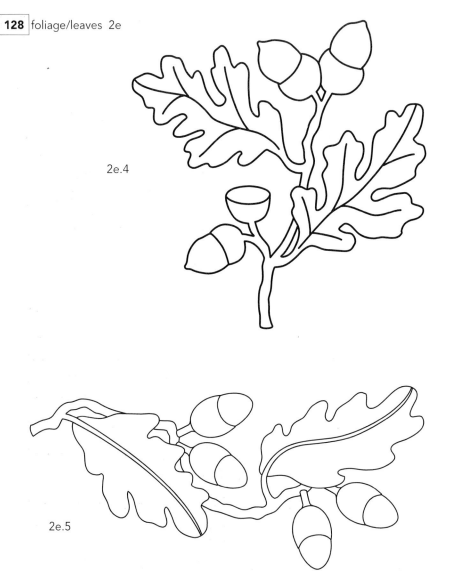

2e.4

2e.5

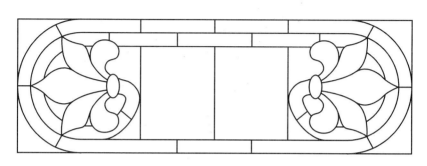

2f.1

2f.2

2f.3

2f.4

2f.5

2f.6

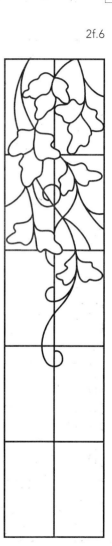

2g.1

2g.2

2g.3

2g.4

2h.1

2h.2

2h.3

2h.4

2h.5

2h.6

2i.1

2i.2

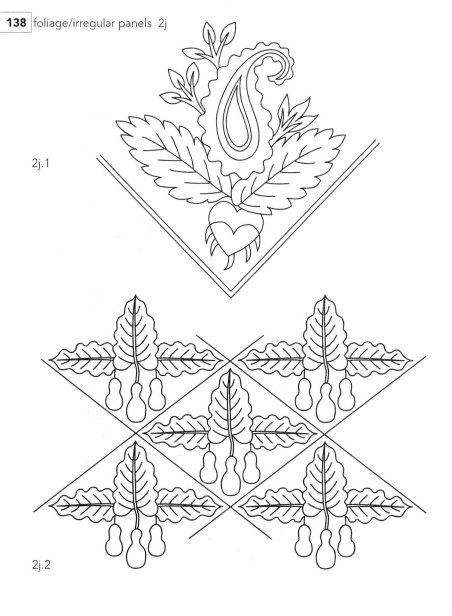

2j.1

2j.2

2j.3

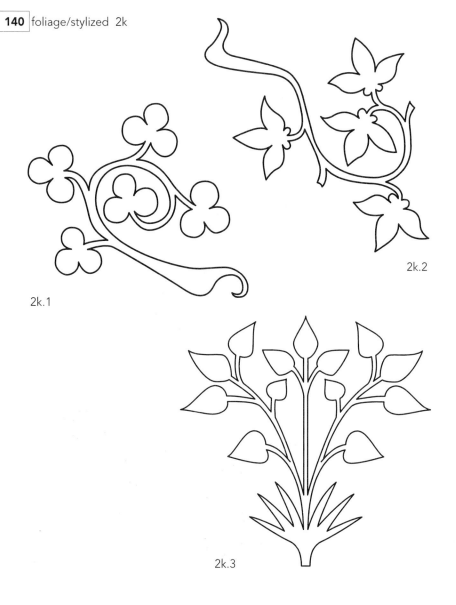

2k.1

2k.2

2k.3

2k.4

2k.5

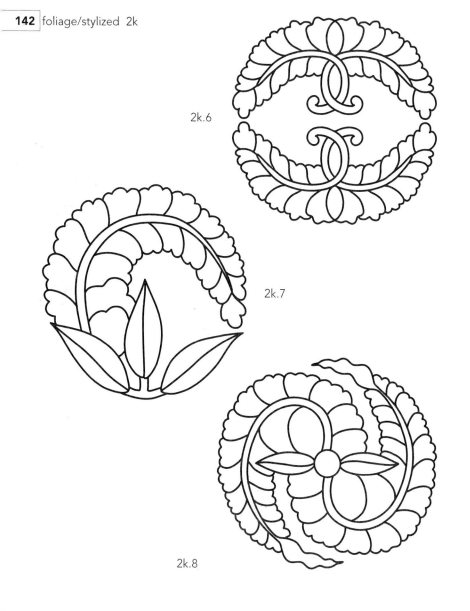

2k.6

2k.7

2k.8

2k.9

2k.10

2k.11

2k.12

2k.13

2k.14

2k.15

2k.16

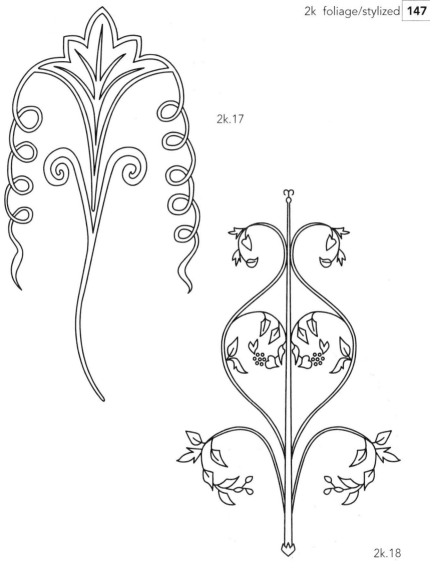

2k.17

2k.18

2k.19

2k.20

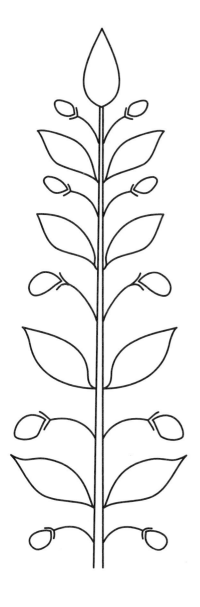

2k.21

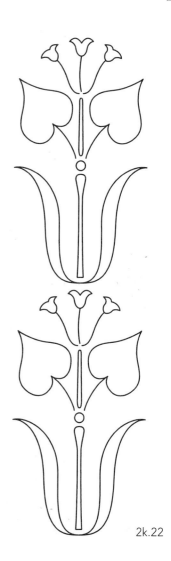

2k.22

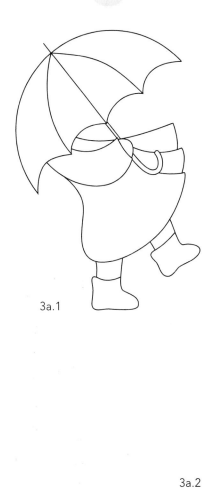

3a.1

3a.2

3a.3

3a.4

3a.5

3b.1

3b.2

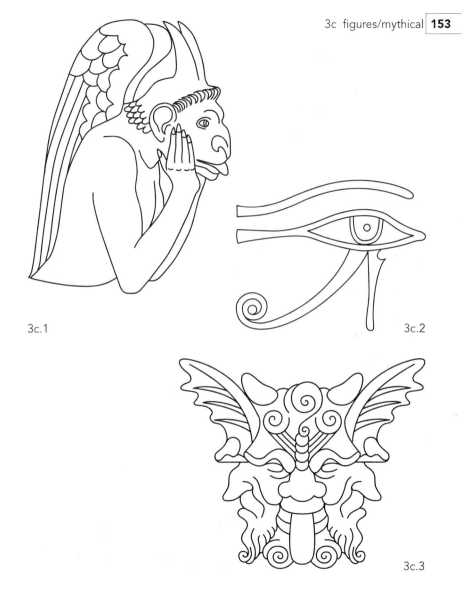

3c.1

3c.2

3c.3

3d.1

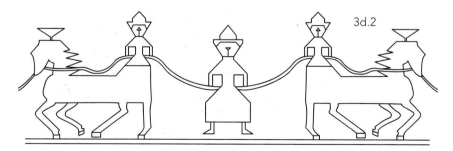

3d.2

3d.3

3e.1

3e.2

3e.3

3e.4

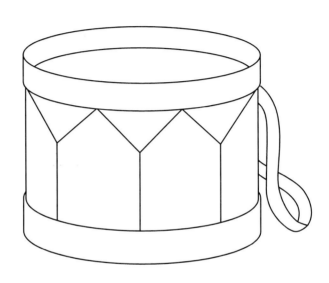

4a.1

4a.2

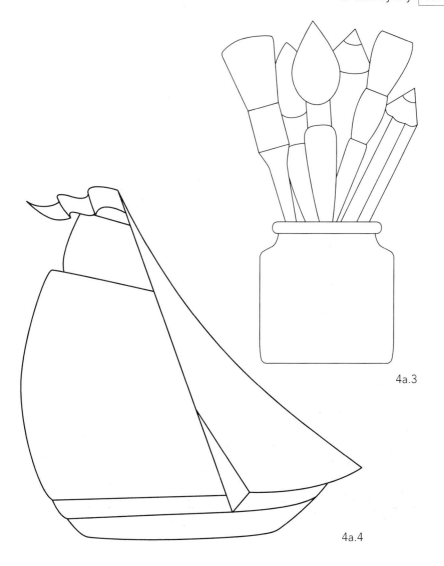

4a.3

4a.4

4a.5

4a.6

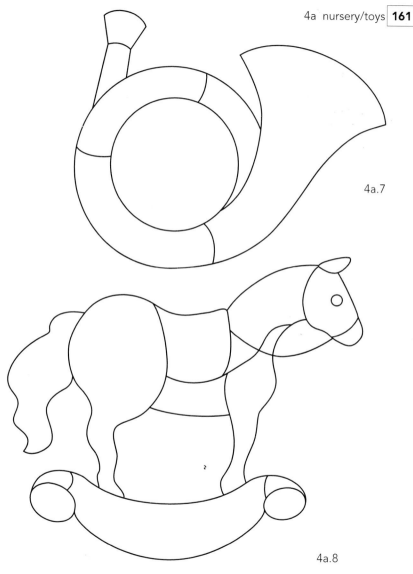

4a.7

4a.8

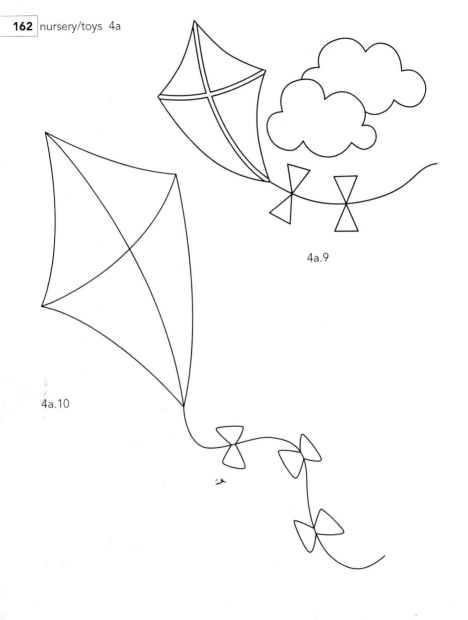

4a.9

4a.10

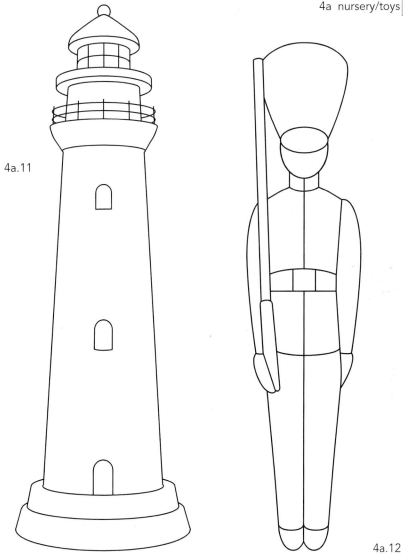

4a.11

4a.12

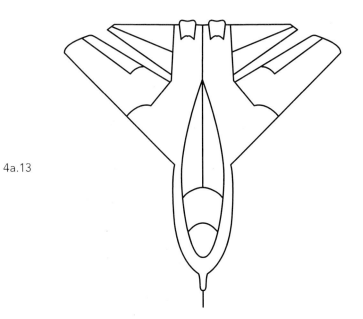

4a.13

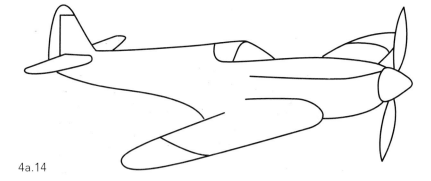

4a.14

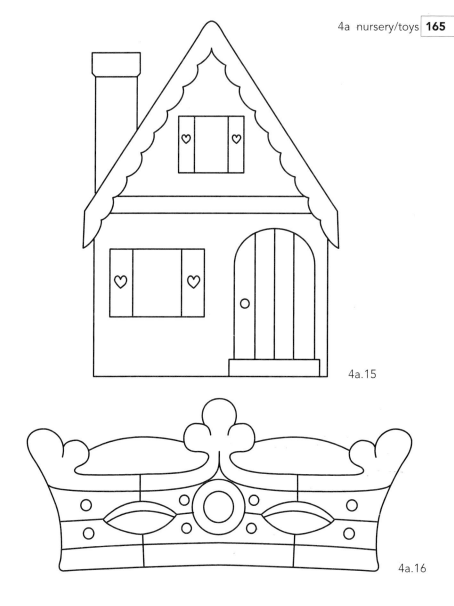

4a.15

4a.16

4b.1

4b.2

4b.3

4b.4

4c.1

4c.2

4c.3

4c.4

4c.5

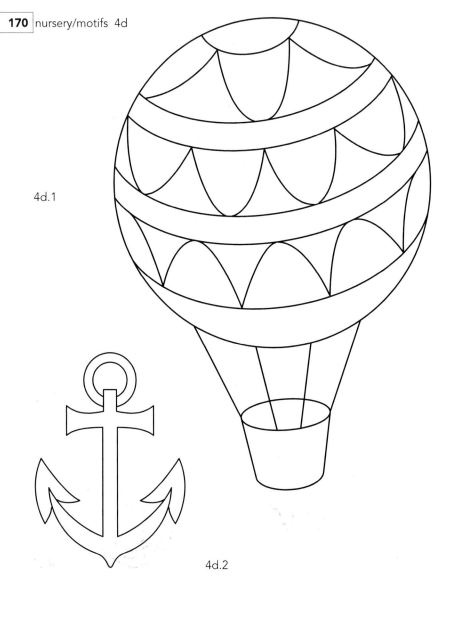

4d.1

4d.2

4d.3

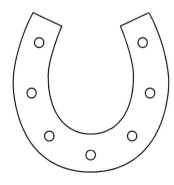

4d.4

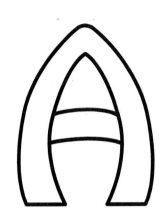

5a.1

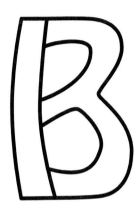

5a.2

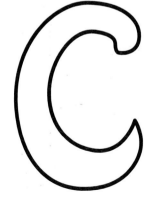

5a.3

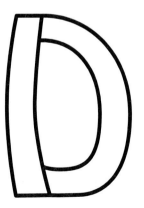

5a.4

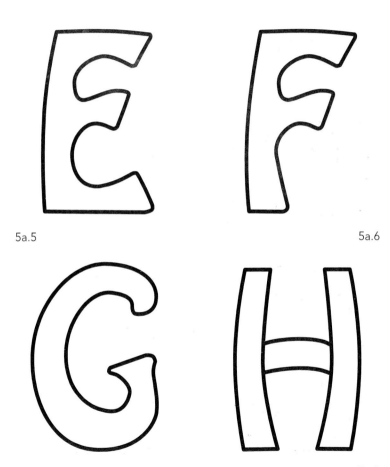

5a.5

5a.6

5a.7

5a.8

5a.9

5a.10

5a.11

5a.12

5a.13

5a.14

5a.15

5a.16

5a.17

5a.18

5a.19

5a.20

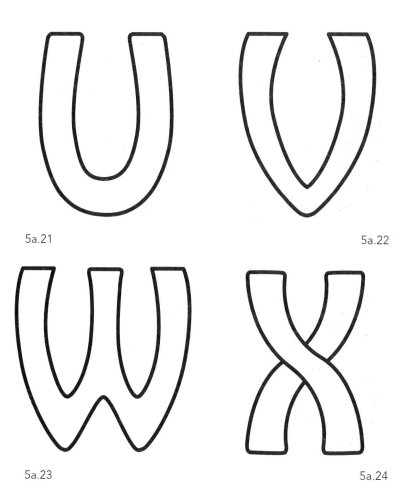

5a.21

5a.22

5a.23

5a.24

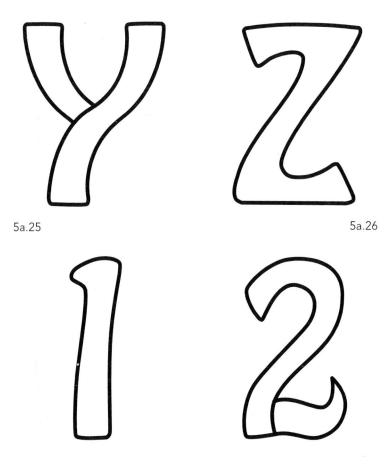

5a.25

5a.26

5b.1

5b.2

5b.3

5b.4

5b.5

5b.6

5b.7

5b.8

5b.9

5b.10

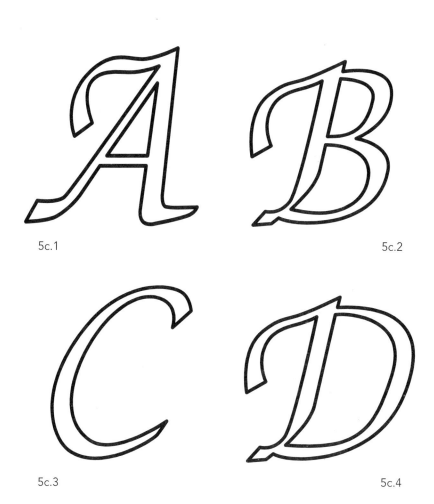

5c.1

5c.2

5c.3

5c.4

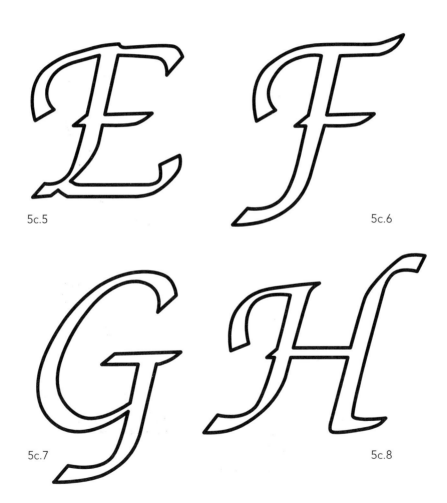

5c.5

5c.6

5c.7

5c.8

5c.9

5c.10

5c.11

5c.12

5c.13

5c.14

5c.15

5c.16

5c.17

5c.18

5c.19

5c.20

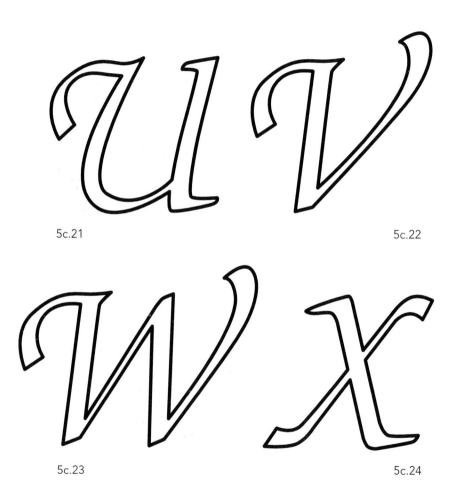

5c.21

5c.22

5c.23

5c.24

5c.25

5c.26

5d.1

5d.2

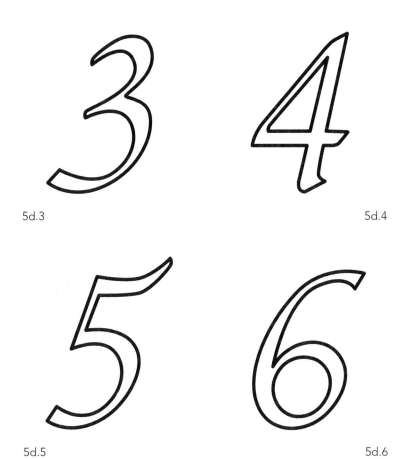

5d.3

5d.4

5d.5

5d.6

5d.7

5d.8

5d.9

5d.10

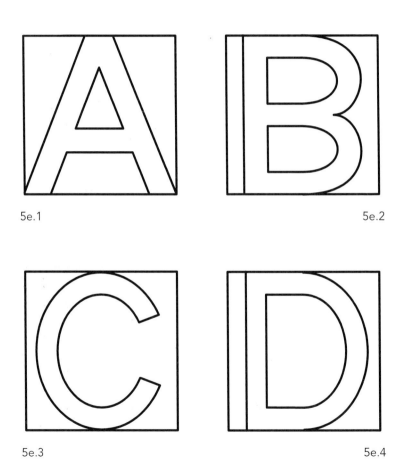

5e.1

5e.2

5e.3

5e.4

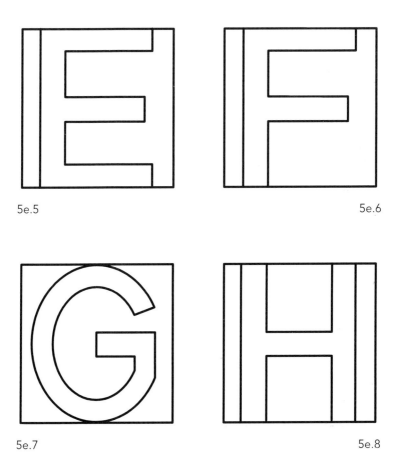

5e.5

5e.6

5e.7

5e.8

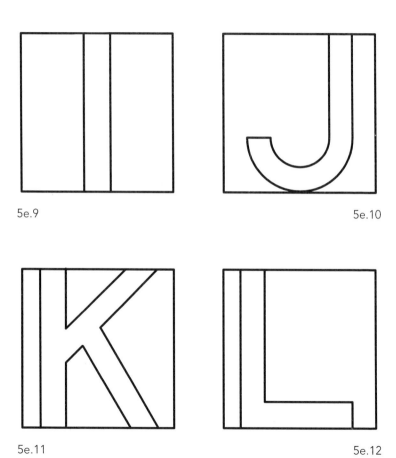

5e.9

5e.10

5e.11

5e.12

5e.13

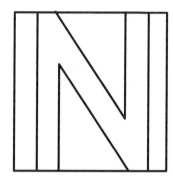

5e.14

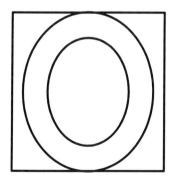

5e.15

5e.16

5e.17

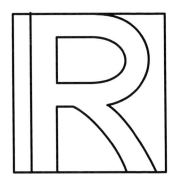

5e.18

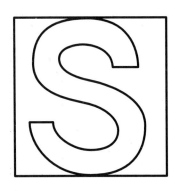

5e.19

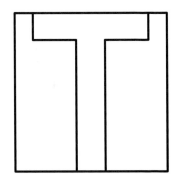

5e.20

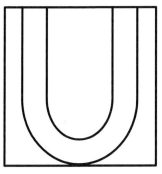

5e.21

5e.22

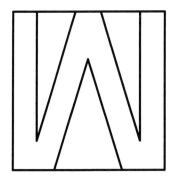

5e.23

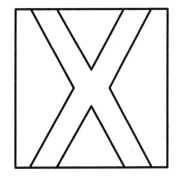

5e.24

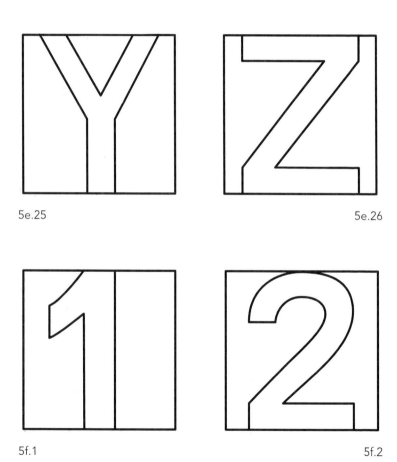

5e.25

5e.26

5f.1

5f.2

5f.3

5f.4

5f.5

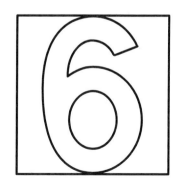

5f.6

5f.7

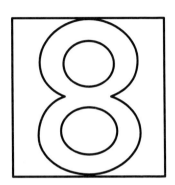

5f.8

5f.9

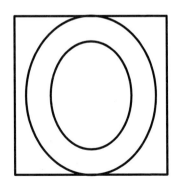

5f.10

If you are outlining lettering onto the back of a piece of glass then you will need to reverse the letters, so that when they are seen from the front they are the right way round. To do this, photocopy the letters you want to outline, lay them face down on a sheet of white paper and trace over the back of the lines with a pen. The result should look like the letters on this page. Use the reversed templates in the usual way (see page 3).

5g.1

5g.2

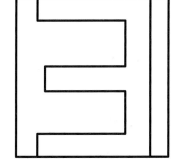

5g.3

6a.1

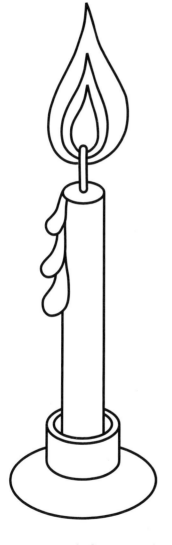

6a.2

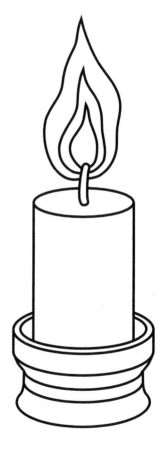

6a.3

6b.1

6b.2

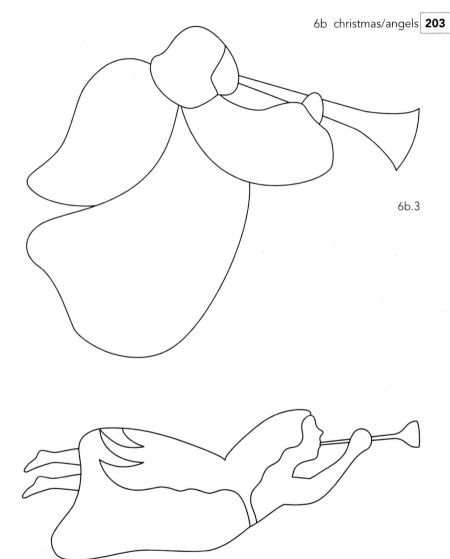

6b.3

6b.4

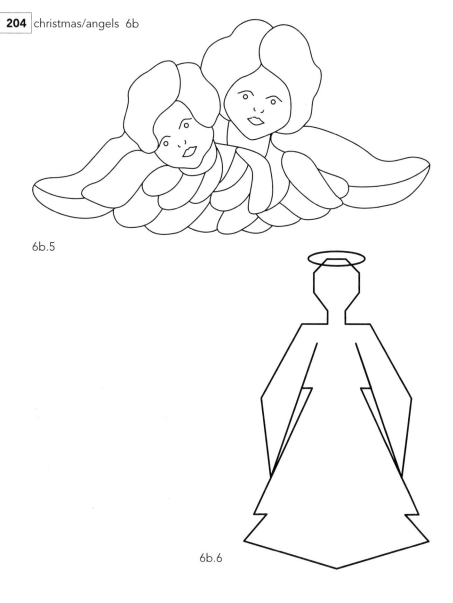

6b.5

6b.6

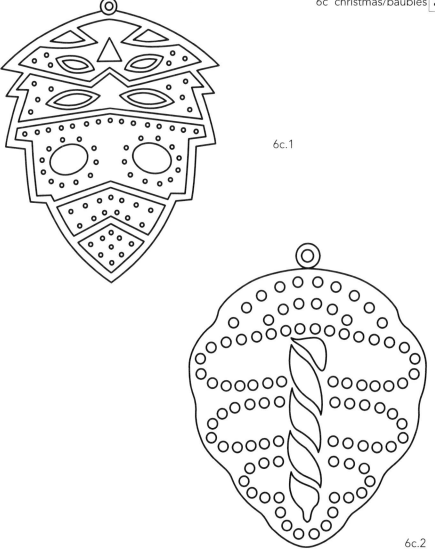

6c.1

6c.2

6c.3

6c.4

6c.5

6d.1

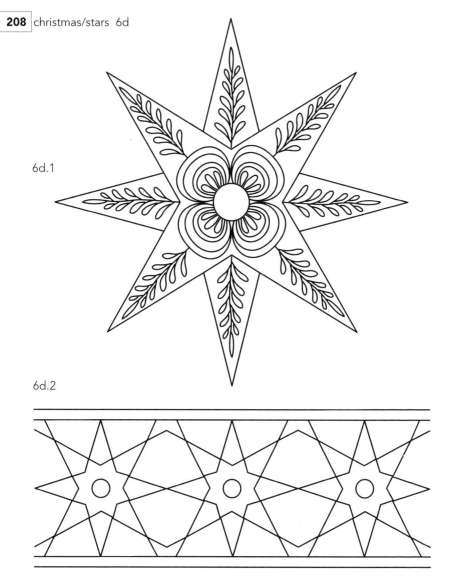

6d.2

6d.3

6d.4

6e.1

6e.2

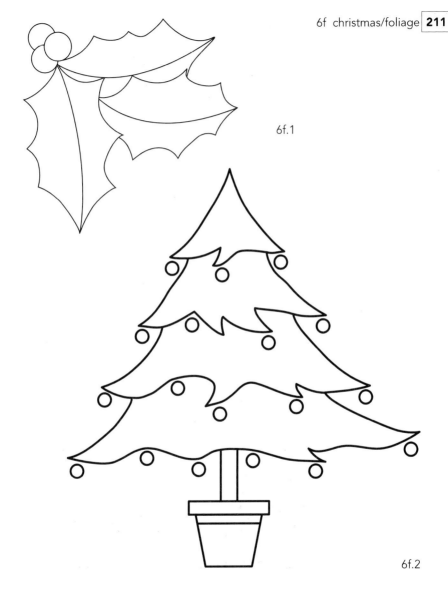

6f.1

6f.2

6g.1

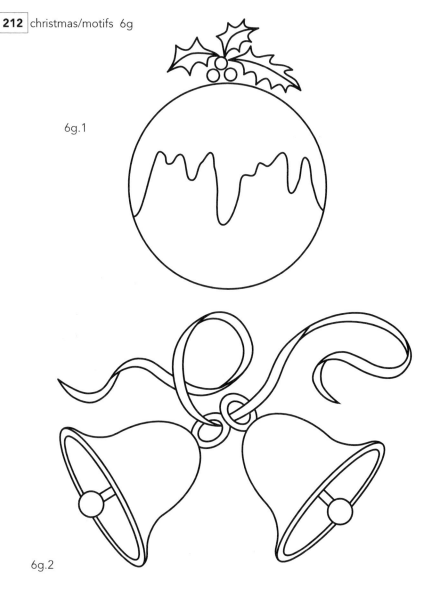

6g.2

6g.3

6g.4

7a.1

7a.2

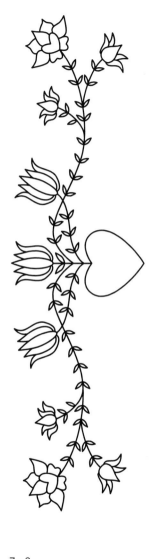

7a.3

7a.4

7a.5

7a.6

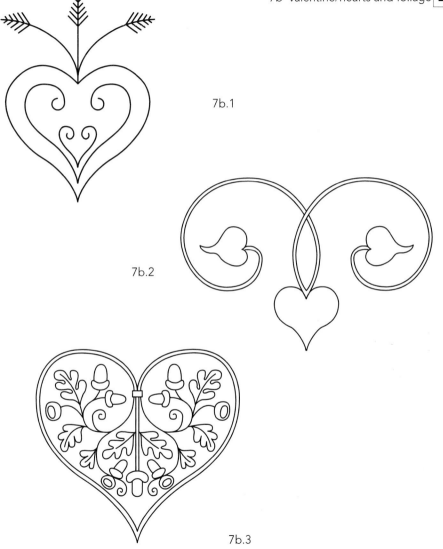

7b.1

7b.2

7b.3

7c.1

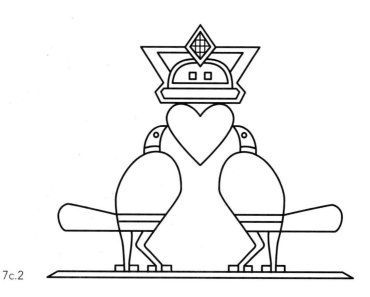

7c.2

7d.1

7d.2

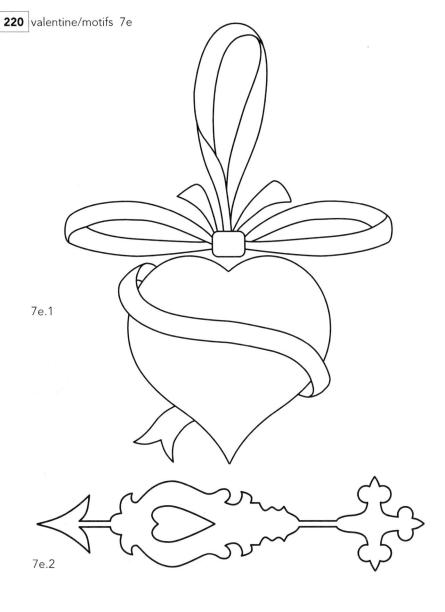

7e.1

7e.2

7e.3

7e.4

8a.1

8a.2

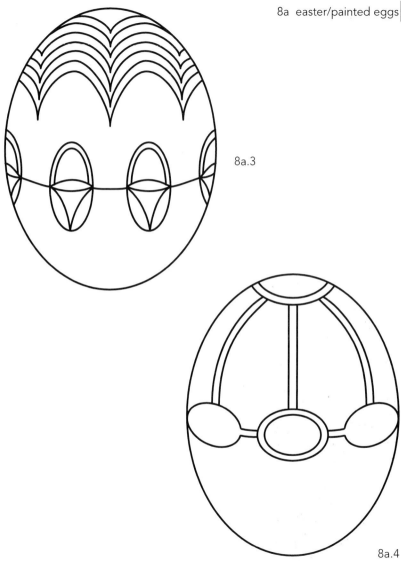

8a.3

8a.4

8a.5

8a.6

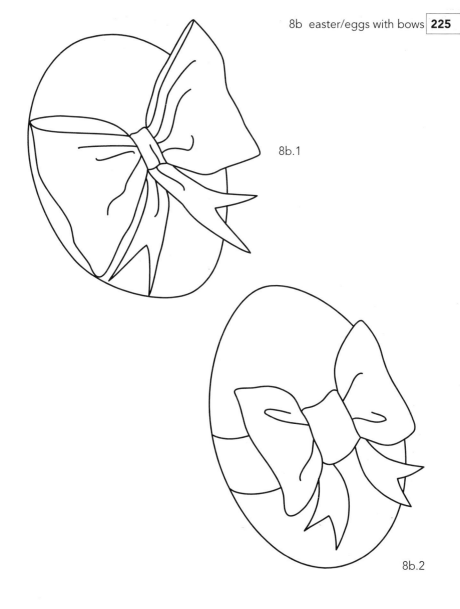

8b.1

8b.2

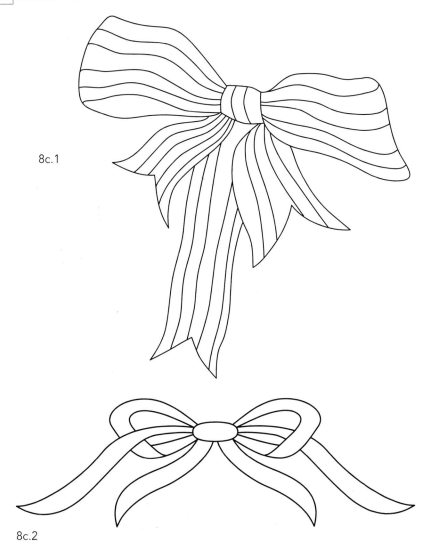

8c.1

8c.2

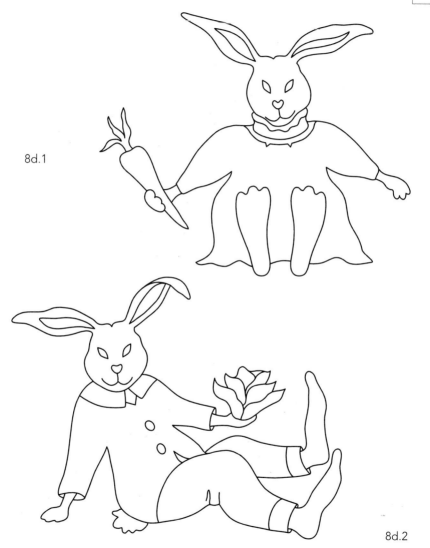

8d.1

8d.2

9a.1

9a.2

9a.3

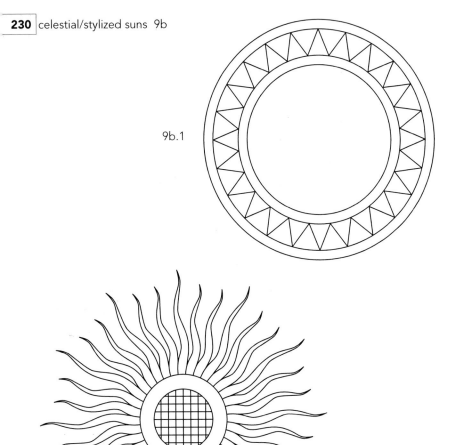

9b.1

9b.2

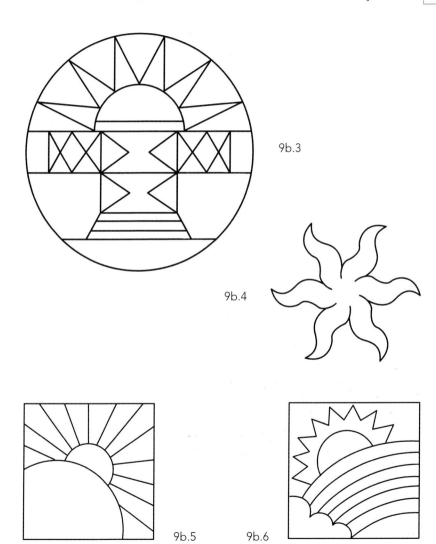

9b.3

9b.4

9b.5

9b.6

9c.1

9c.2

9c.3

9c.4

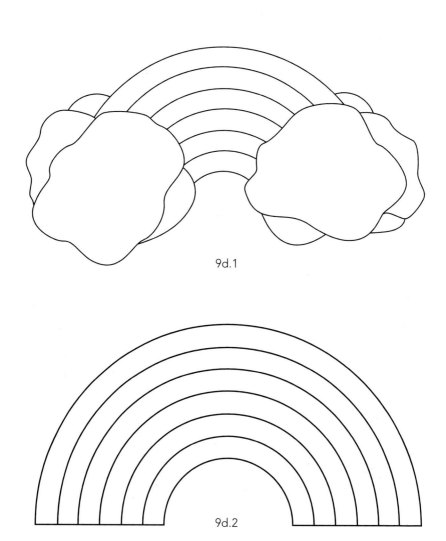

9d.1

9d.2

9e.1

9e.2

9f.1

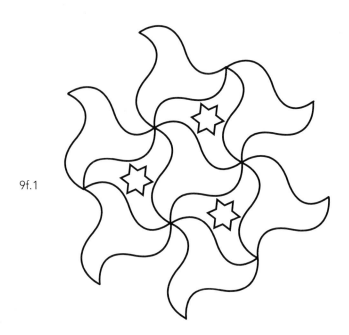

9f.2

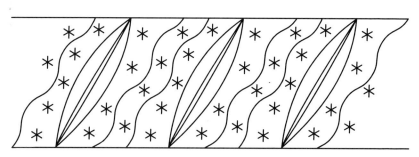

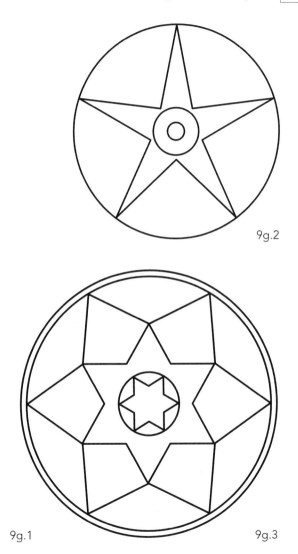

9g.2

9g.1

9g.3

10a.1

10a.2

10a.3

10b.1

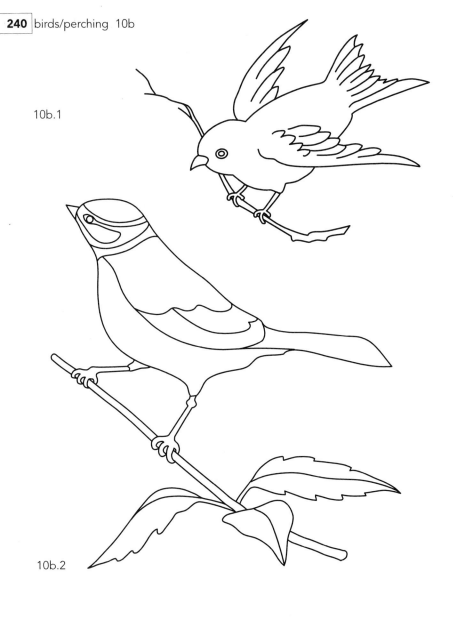

10b.2

10b.3

10b.4

10c.1

10c.2

10c.3

10c.4

10d.1

10d.2

10d.3

10e.1

10e.2

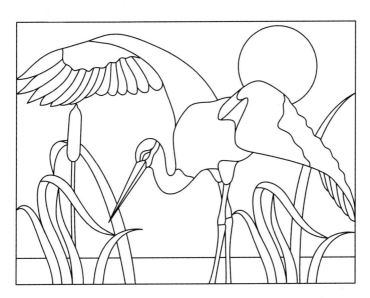

10e.3

10e.4

10e.5

10e.6

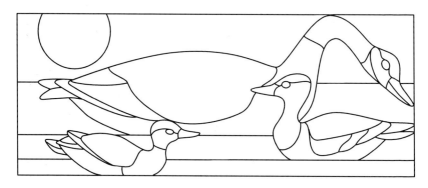

10f.1

10f.2

10f.3

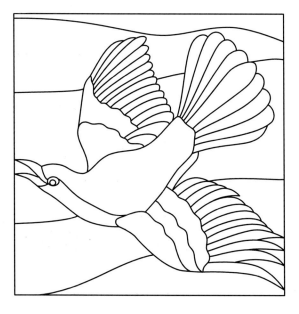

10f.4

10f.5

10f.6

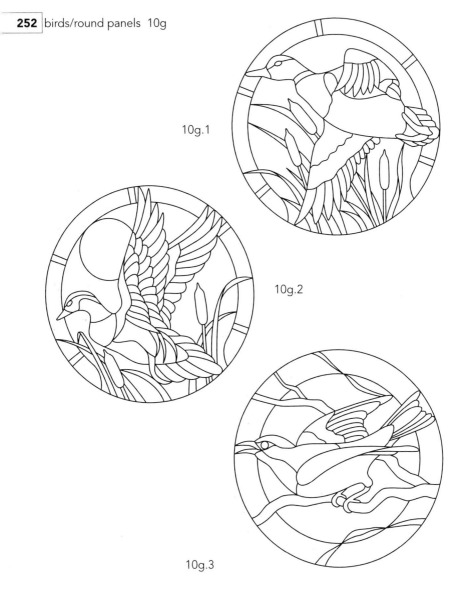

10g.1

10g.2

10g.3

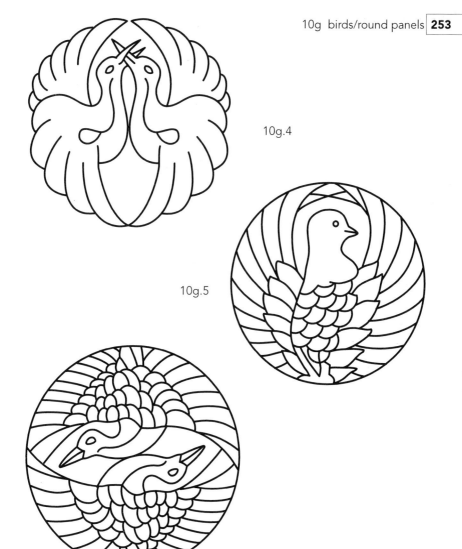

10g.4

10g.5

10g.6

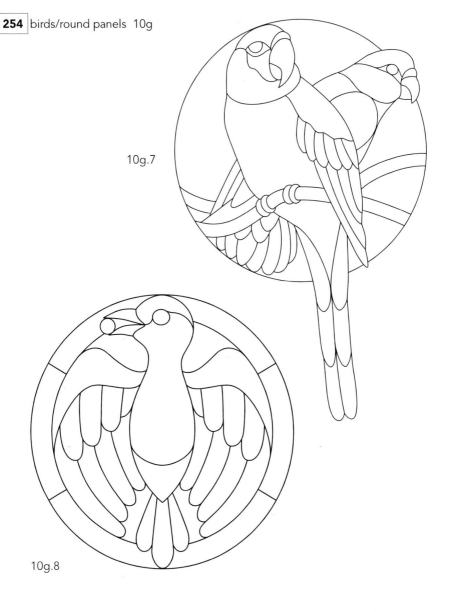

10g.7

10g.8

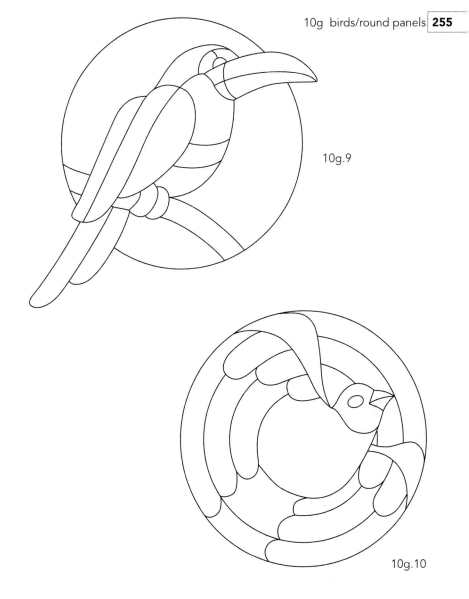

10g.9

10g.10

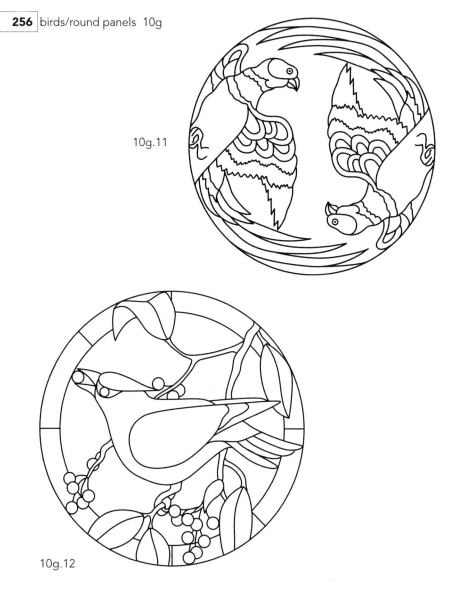

10g.11

10g.12

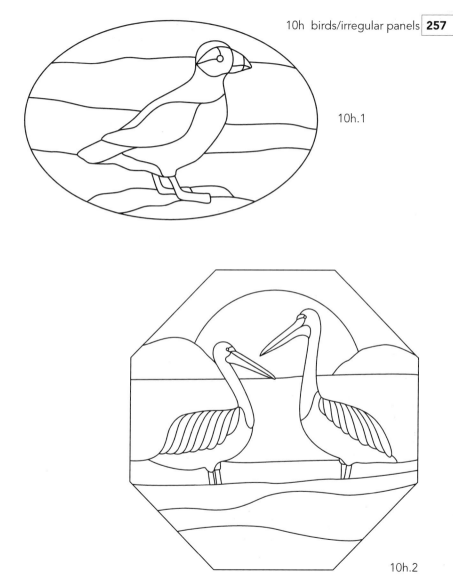

10h.1

10h.2

10h.3

10h.4

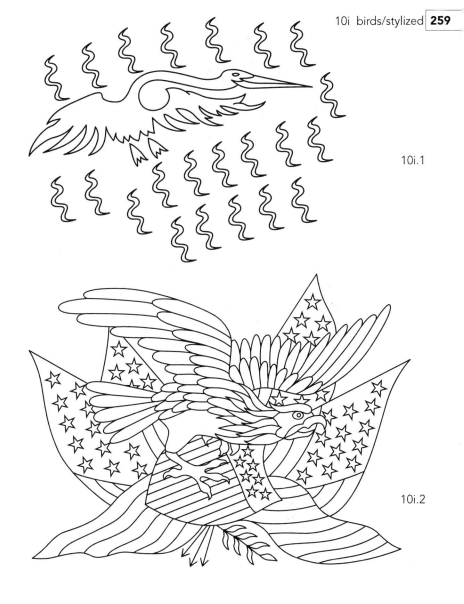

10i.1

10i.2

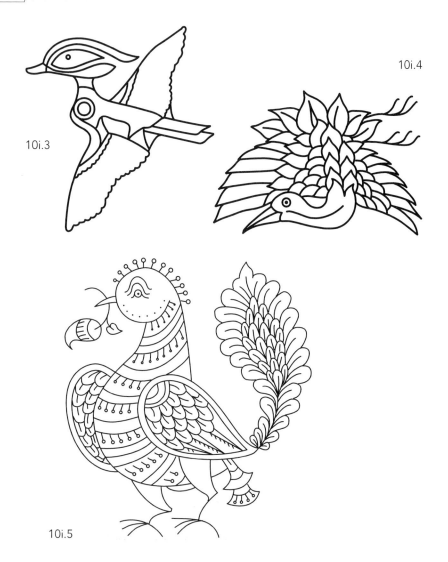

10i.4

10i.3

10i.5

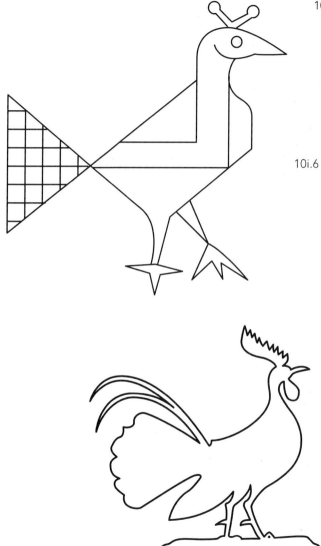

10i.6

10i.7

10i.8

10i.9

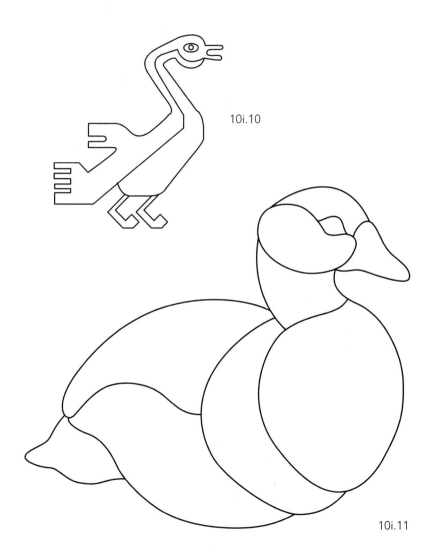

10i.10

10i.11

10j.1

10j.2

10j.3

10j.4

10k.1

10k.2

10k.3

10k.4

10k.5

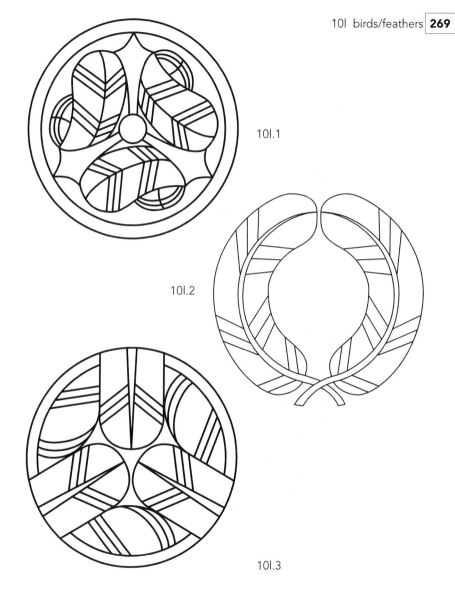

10l.1

10l.2

10l.3

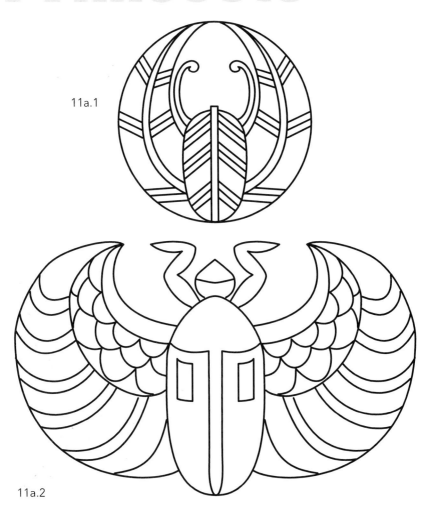

11a.1

11a.2

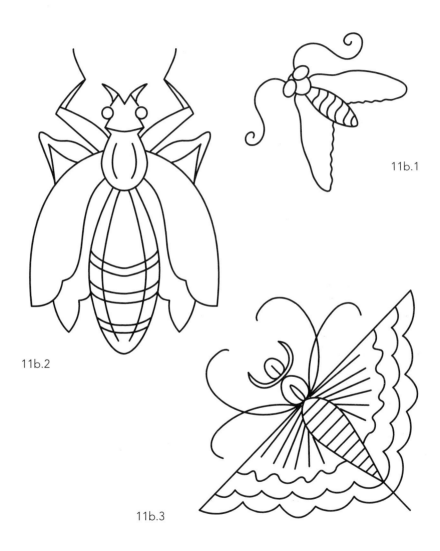

11b.1

11b.2

11b.3

11c.1

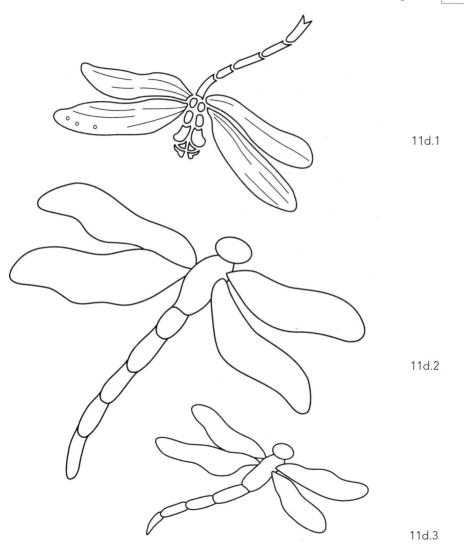

11d.1

11d.2

11d.3

11e.1

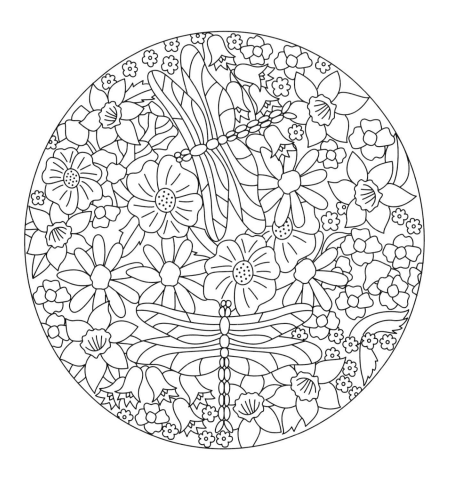

11e.2

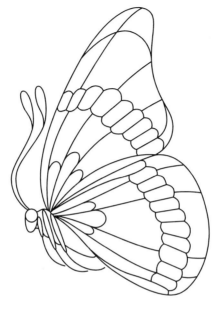

11f.1

11f.2

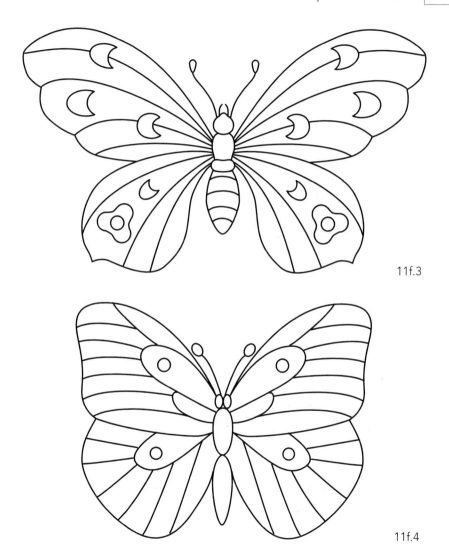

11f.3

11f.4

11f.5

11f.6

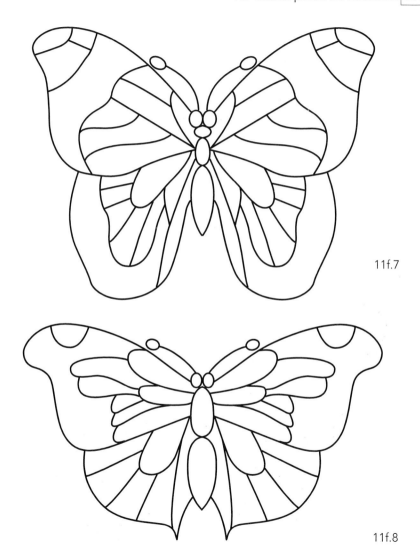

11f.7

11f.8

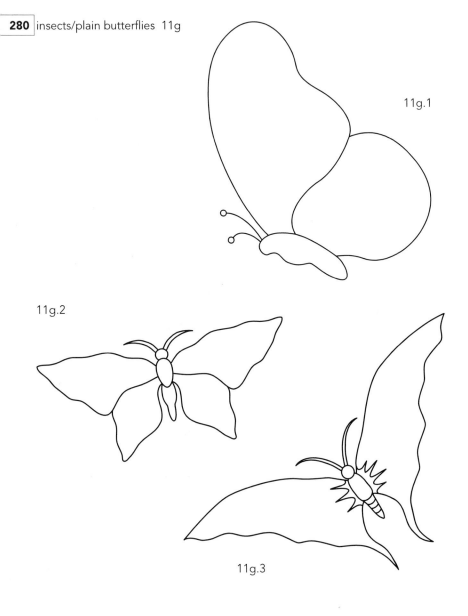

11g.1

11g.2

11g.3

11h.1

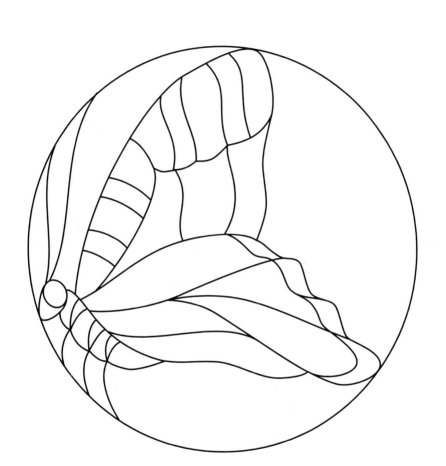

11h.2

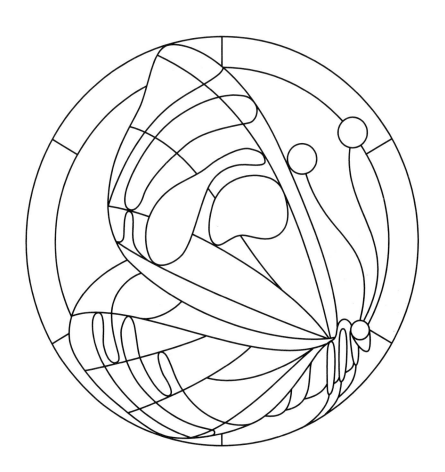

11h.3

11i.1

11i.2

11i.3

11i.4

12a.2

12a.1

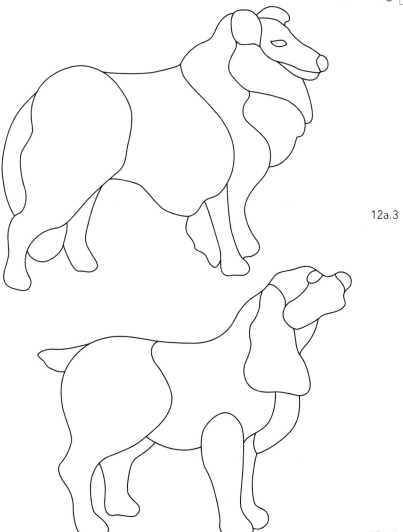

12a.3

12a.4

12b.1

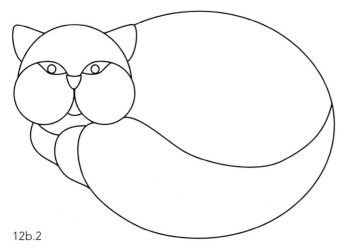

12b.2

12b.3

12c.1

12c.2

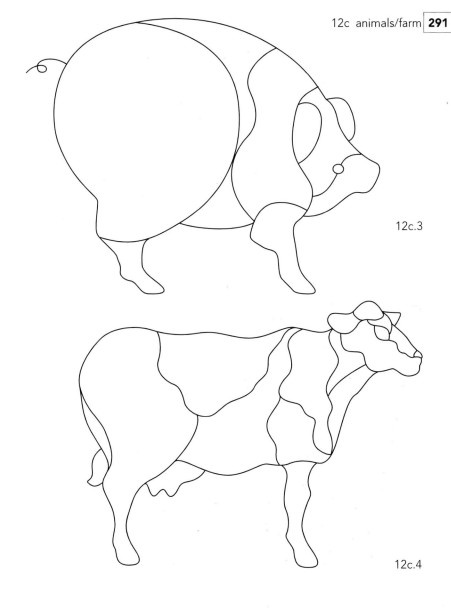

12c.3

12c.4

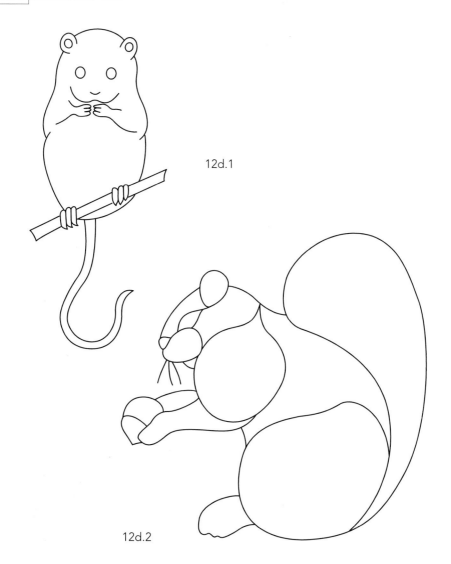

12d.1

12d.2

12d.3

12d.4

12e.1

12e.2

12e.3

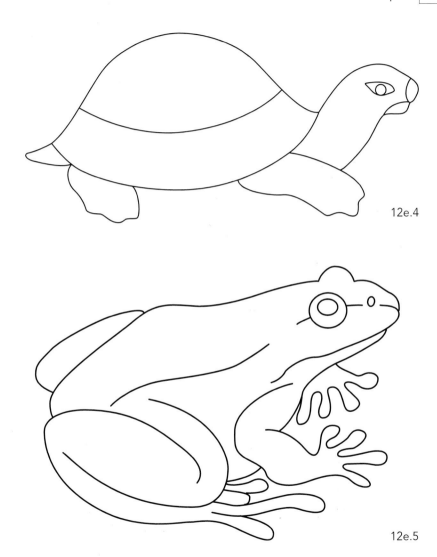

12e.4

12e.5

12f.1

12f.2

12g.1

12g.2

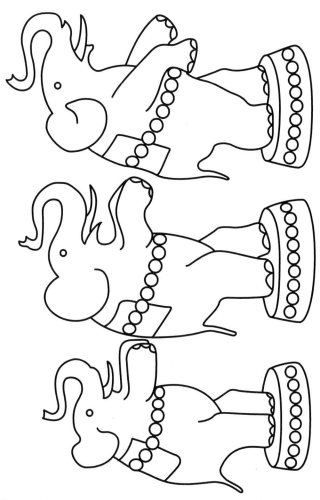

12g.3

12h.1

12h.2

12i.1

12i.2

12i.3

12i.4

12i.5

12i.6

12i.7

12i.8

12i.9

12j.1

12j.2

12j.3

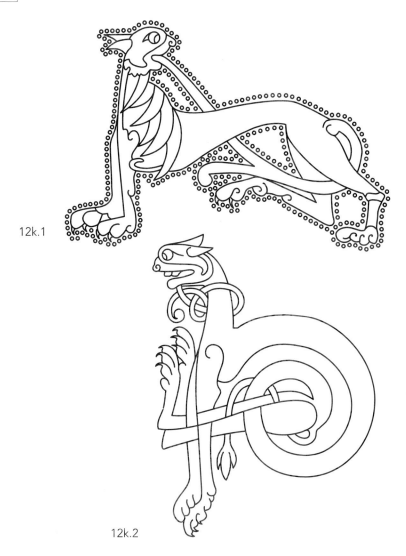

12k.1

12k.2

12l.1

12l.2

12m.1

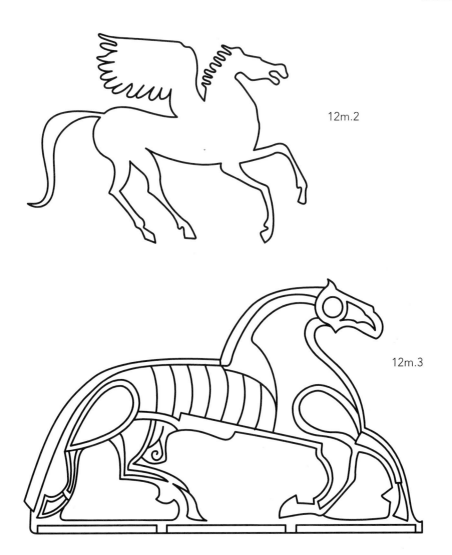

12m.2

12m.3

12n.1

12n.2

12n.3

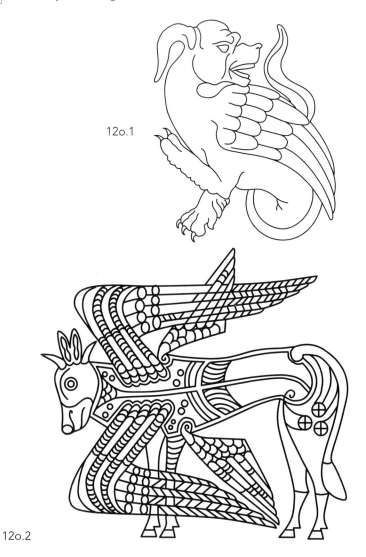

12o.1

12o.2

12o.3

12o.4

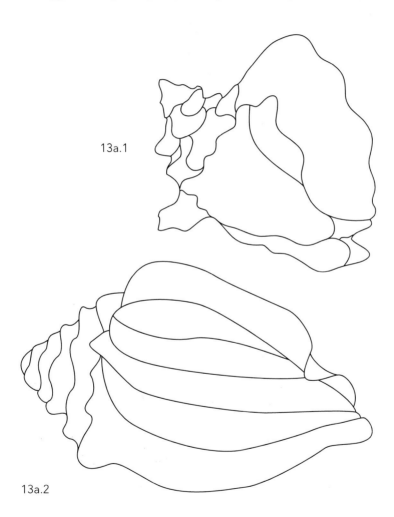

13a.1

13a.2

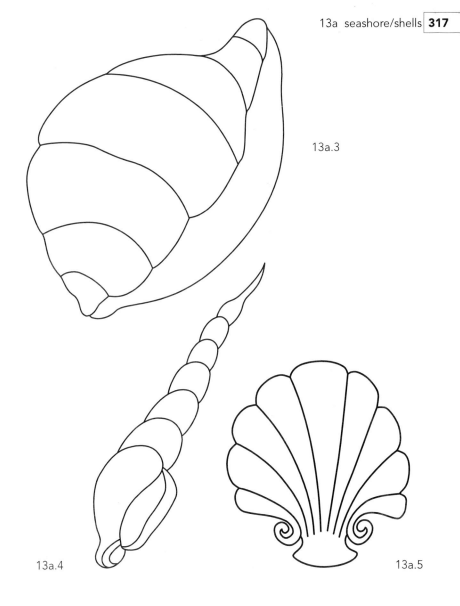

13a.3

13a.4

13a.5

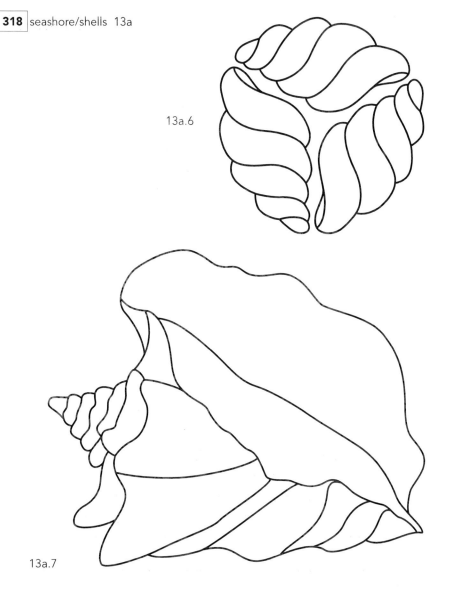

13a.6

13a.7

13b.1

13c.1

13c.2

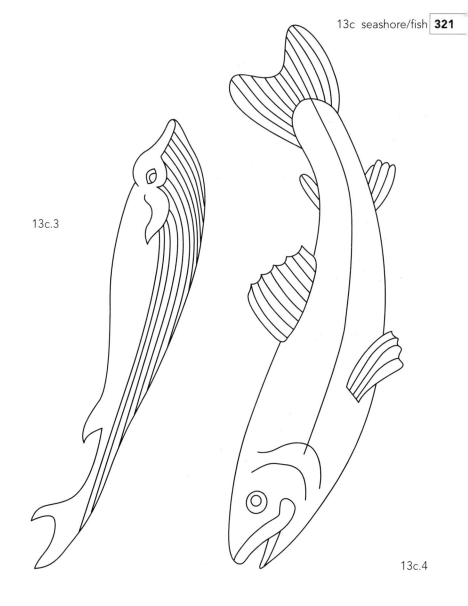

13c.3

13c.4

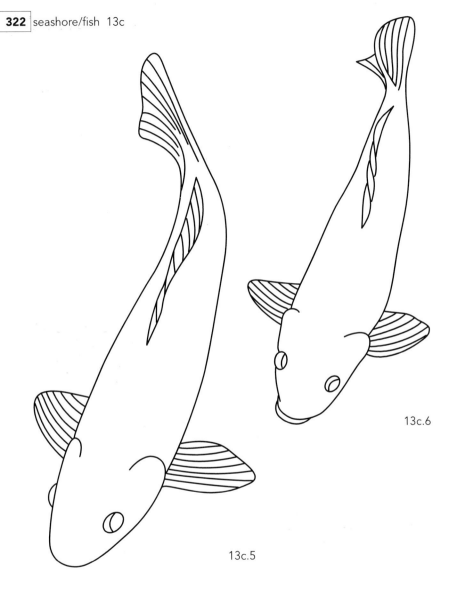

13c.6

13c.5

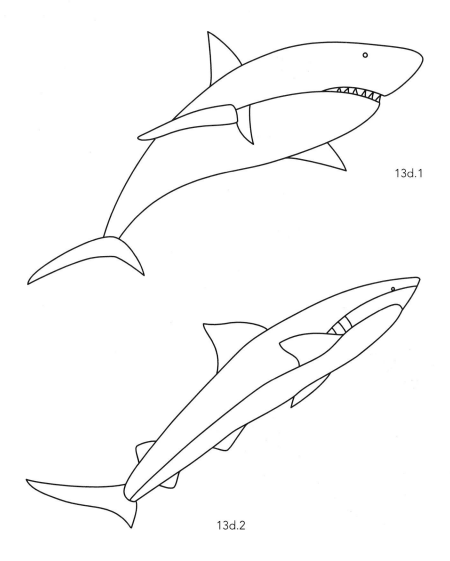

13d.1

13d.2

13e.1

13e.2

13f.1

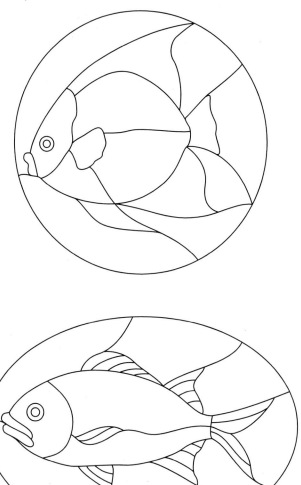

13f.2

13f.3

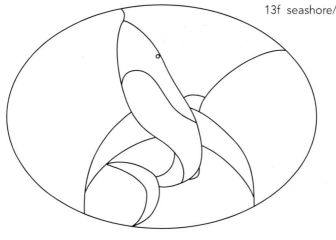

13f.4

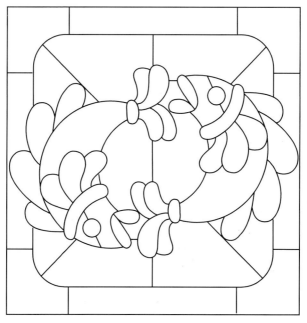

13f.5

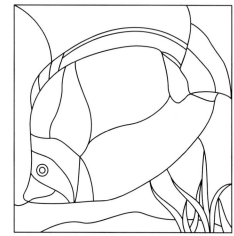

13f.6

13f.7

13f.8

13f.9

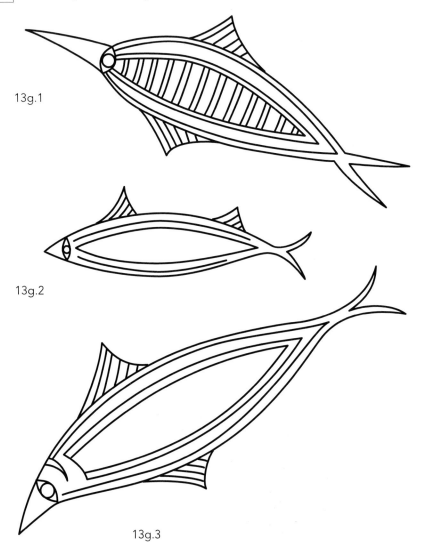

13g.1

13g.2

13g.3

13h.1

13i.1

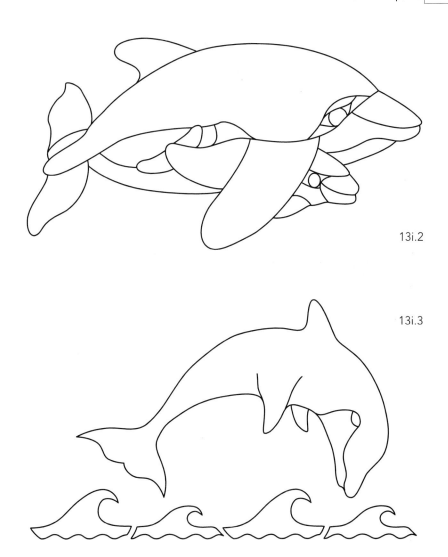

13i.2

13i.3

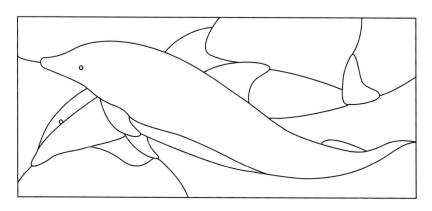

13j.1

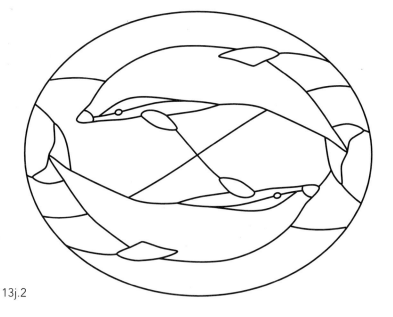

13j.2

13j.3

13k.1

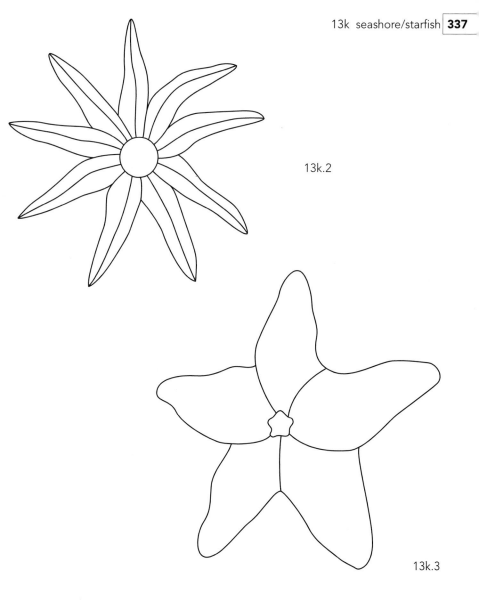

13k.2

13k.3

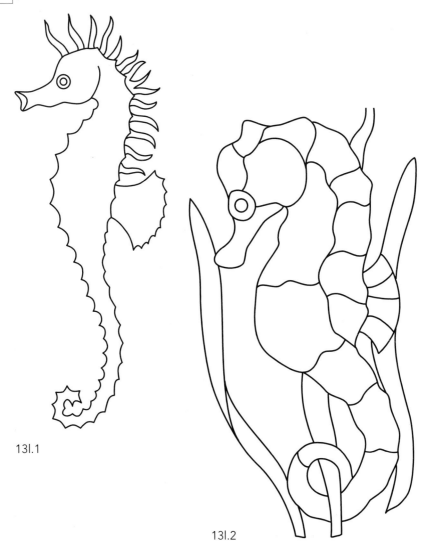

13l.1

13l.2

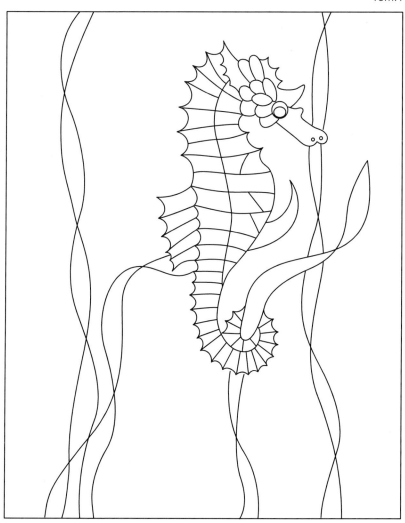

13n.1

13n.2

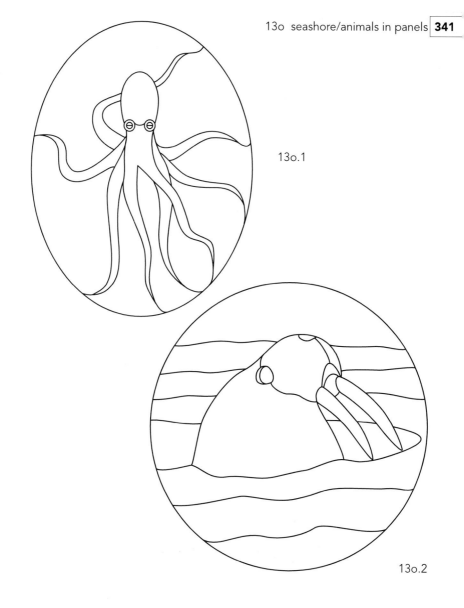

13o.1

13o.2

13p.1

14a.1

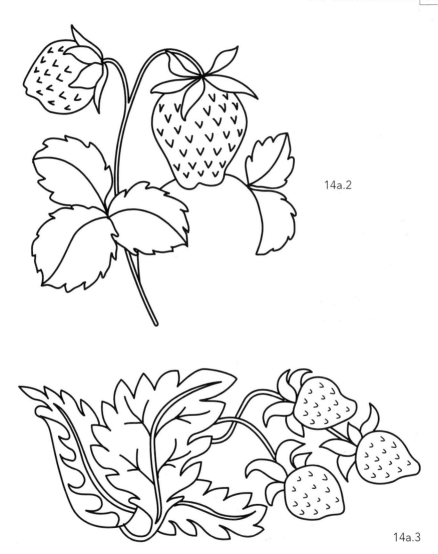

14a.2

14a.3

14b.1

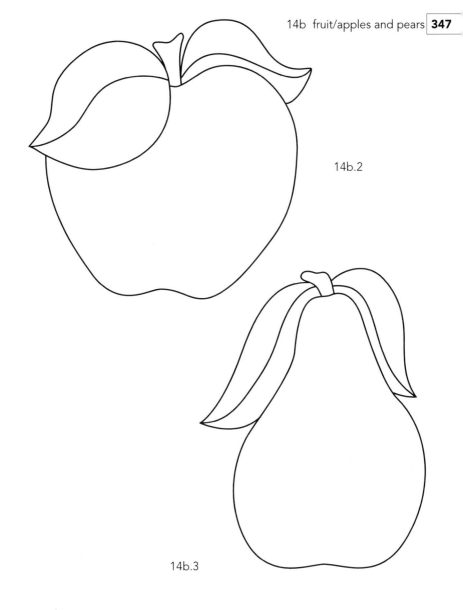

14b.2

14b.3

14b.4

14b.5

14c.1

14c.2

14d.1

14d.2

14d.3

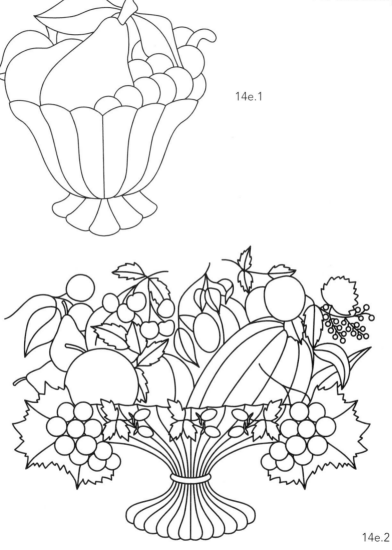

14e.1

14e.2

14f.1

14f.2

14f.3

14f.4

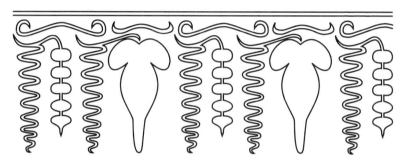

14g.1

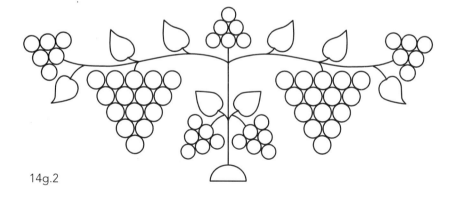

14g.2

14g.3

14g.4

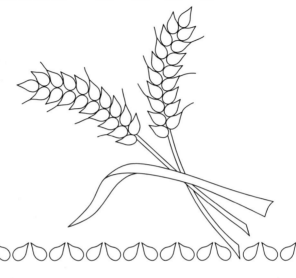

15a.1

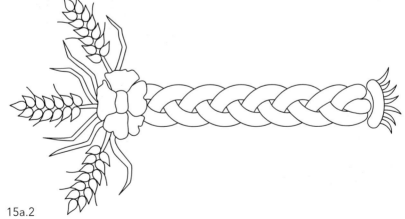

15a.2

15b.1                                        15b.2

15c.1

15c.2

15c.3

15c.4

16.patterns

16a.1

16a.2

16a.3

16a.4

16a.5

16a.6

16a.7

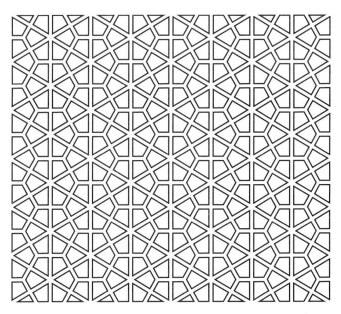

16a.8

16b.1

16b.2

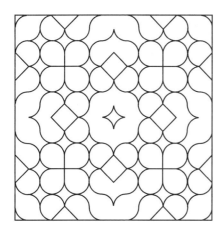

16b.3

16b.4

16c.1

16c.2

16c.3

16c.4

16c.5

16d.1

16d.2

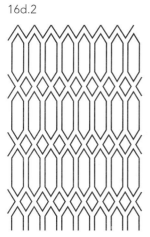

16d.3

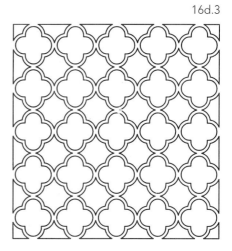

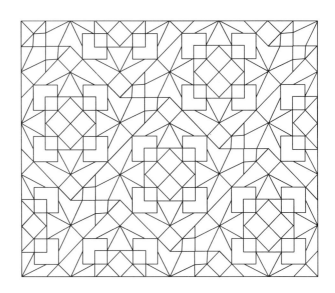

16e.1

16e.2

16e.3

16e.4

16f.1

16f.2

16f.3

16f.4

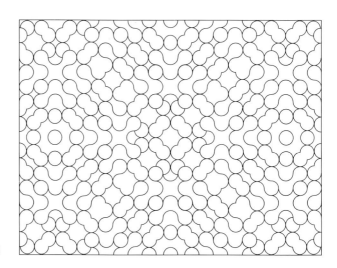

16f.5

16f.6

16f.7

16f.8

17a.2

17a.1

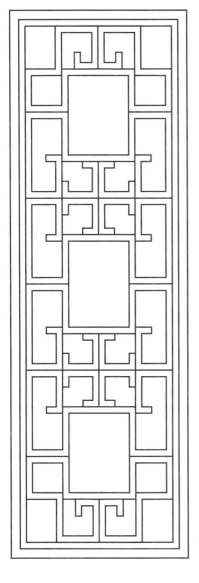

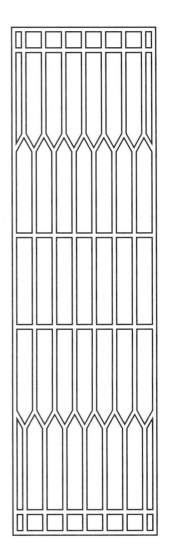

17a.3

17a.4

17a.5

17a.6

17a.7

17a.8

17a.9

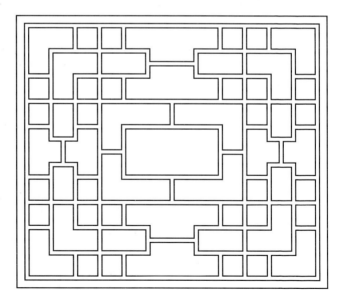

17a.10

17a.11

17a.12

17a.13

17a.14

17b.1

17b.2

17c.2

17c.1

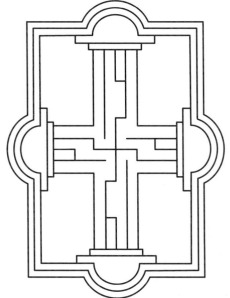

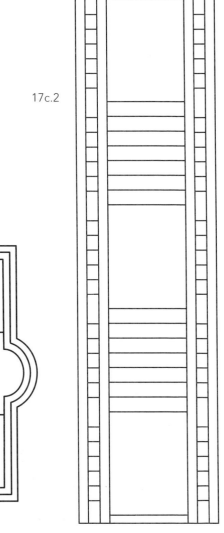

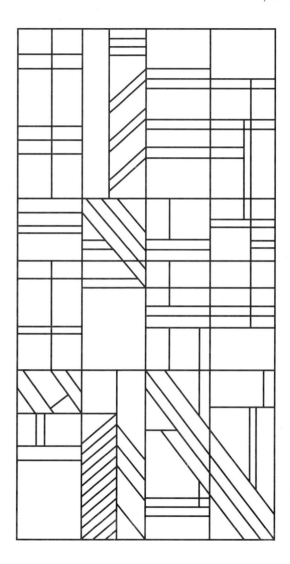

17c.3

17c.4

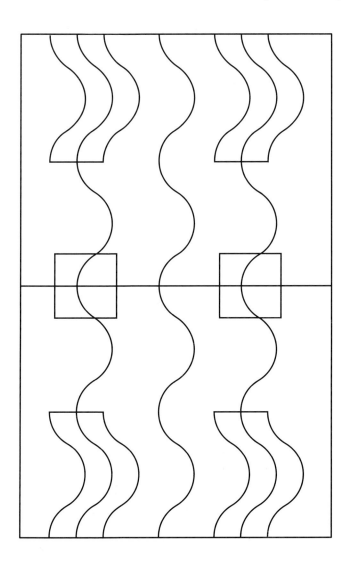

17c.5

17d.1

17d.2

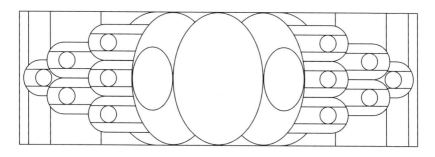

17d.3

17e.1

17e.2

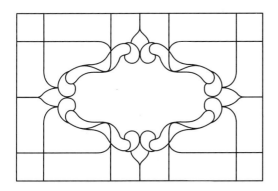

17e.3

17e.4

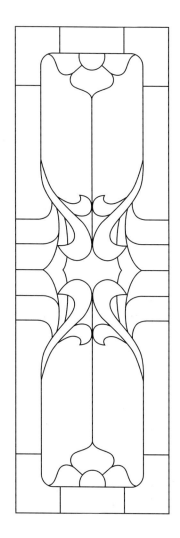

17e.5

17e.6

17e.7

17e.8

17f.1

17f.2

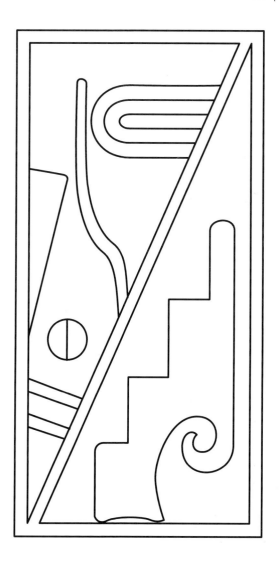

17f.3

17g.1

17g.2

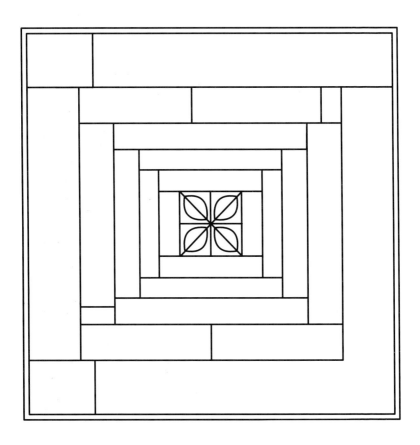

17h.1

17h.2

17h.3

17h.4

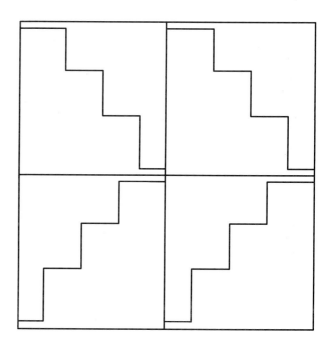

17h.5

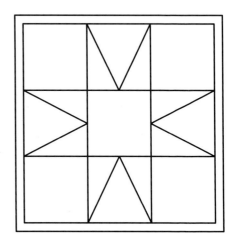

17h.6

17h.7

17i.1

17i.2

17i.3

17j.1

17j.2

17k.1

17k.2

17k.3

17l.1

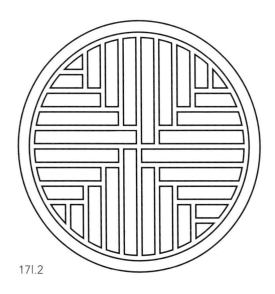

17l.2

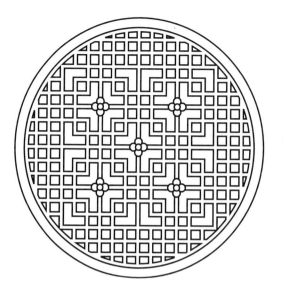

171.3

171.4

171.5

171.6

171.7

17m.1

17m.2

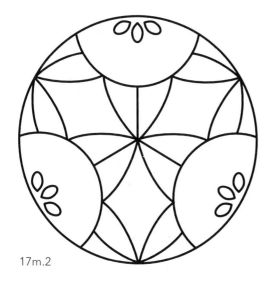

17m.3

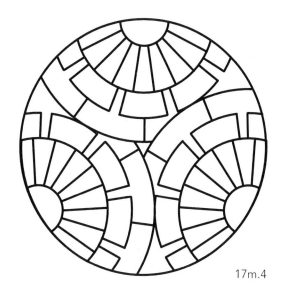

17m.4

17m.5

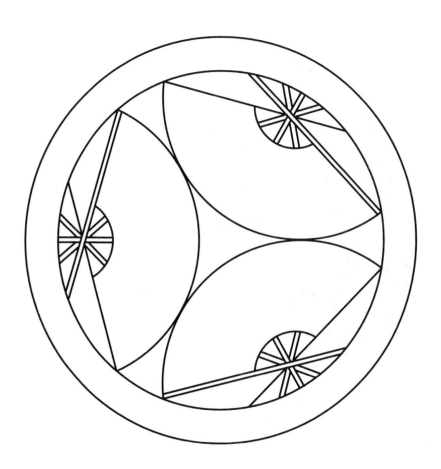

17m.6

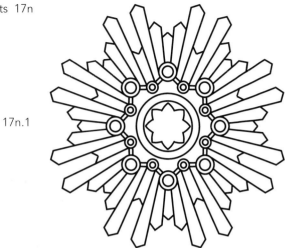

17n.1

17n.2

17n.3

17n.4

17n.5

17n.6

17n.7

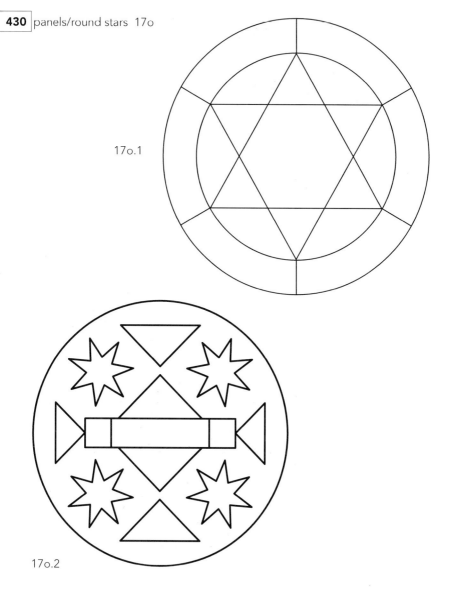

17o.1

17o.2

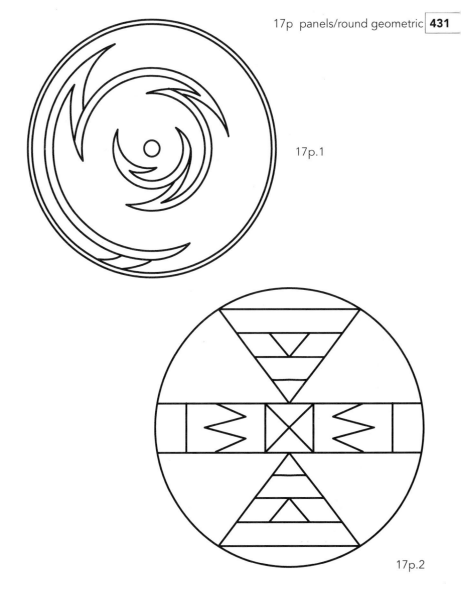

17p.1

17p.2

17q.1

17q.2

17q.3

17q.4

17q.5

17q.6

17q.7

17q.8

17q.9

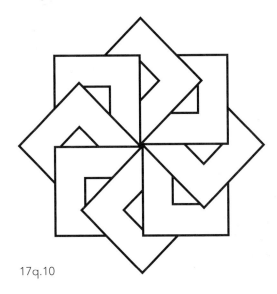

17q.10

17q.11

17q.12

17q.13

17r.1

17r.2

17s.1

17s.2

17s.3

17s.4

17s.5

17s.6

17s.7

17s.8

17t.1

17t.2

17t.3

17u.1

17u.2

17v.1

17v.2

17v.3

17v.4

17w.1

17w.2

17w.3

17w.4

17w.5

17w.6

17w.7

17w.8

17w.9

17w.10

17w.11

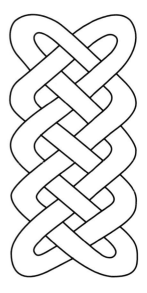

18a.2

18a.1

18b.1

18b.2

18c.1

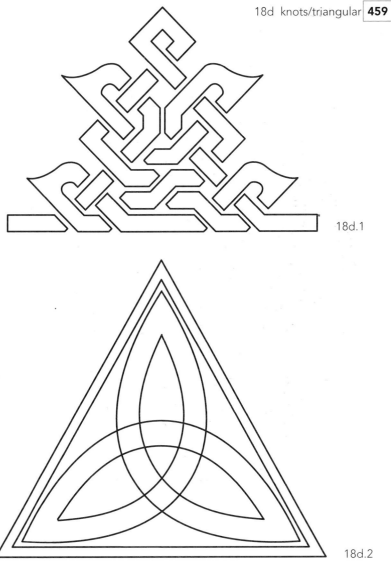

18d.1

18d.2

18e.1

18e.2

18e.3

18f.1

18f.2

18g.1

18g.2

18g.3

# 19.borders

19a.1

19a.2

19a.3

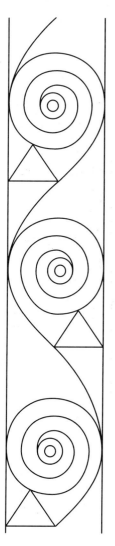

19a.4

19a.5

19a.6

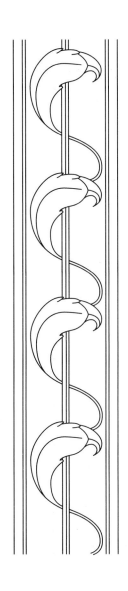

19a.7

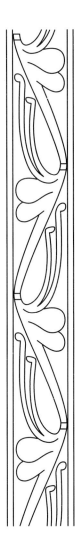

19a.8

19a.9

19b.1

19b.2

19b.3

19b.4

19b.5

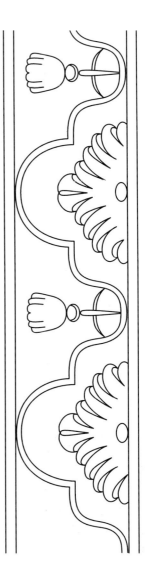

19b.6

19b.7

19b.8                    19b.9

19b.10          19b.11          19b.12

19b.13

19b.14

19b.15

19b.16

19c.1

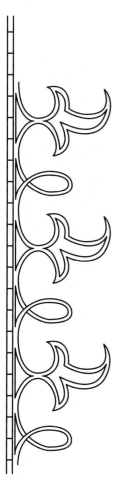

19c.2

19c.3

19c.4

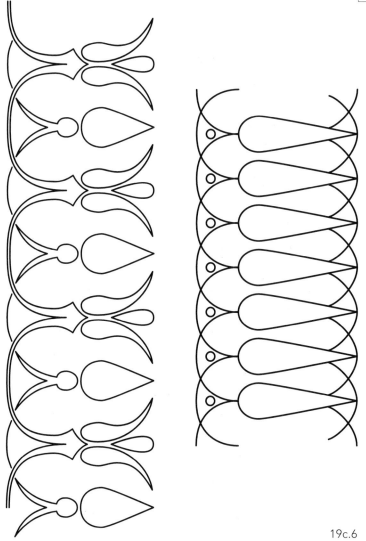

19c.5

19c.6

19c.7

19c.8

19c.9

19c.10

19c.11

19c.12

19c.13

19c.14

19c.15

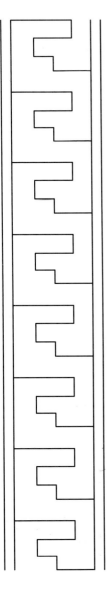

19d.1

19d.2

19d.3

19d.4

19e.1

19e.3

19e.4

19f.2

19f.1

19g.1                              19g.2

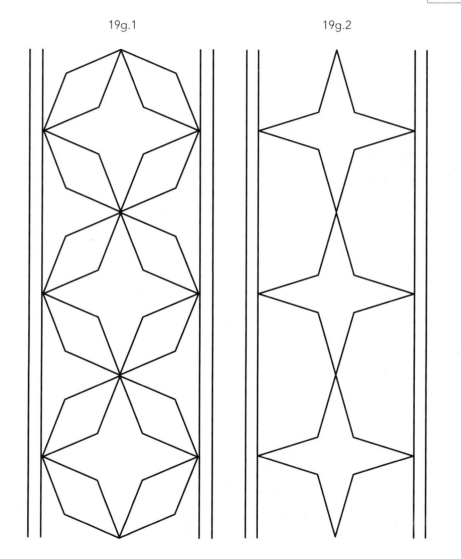

19h.1

19h.2

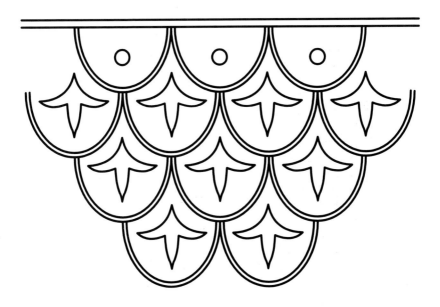

19h.3

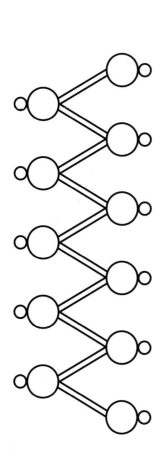

19i.1

19i.2

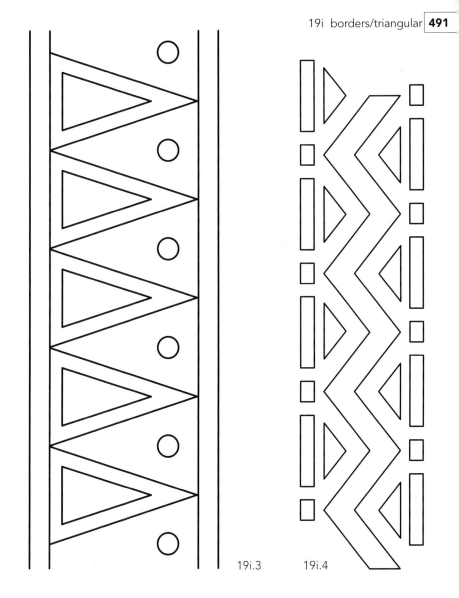

19i.3          19i.4

19j.1

19j.2

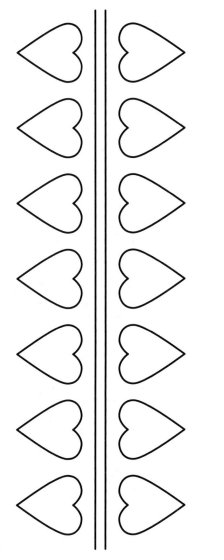

19j.3

19j.4

19j.5

19j.6

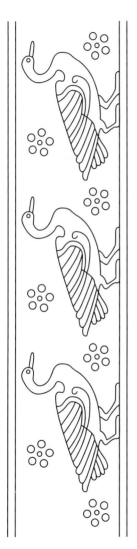

19k.1

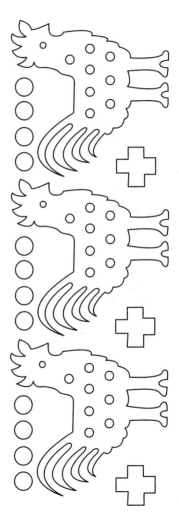

19k.2

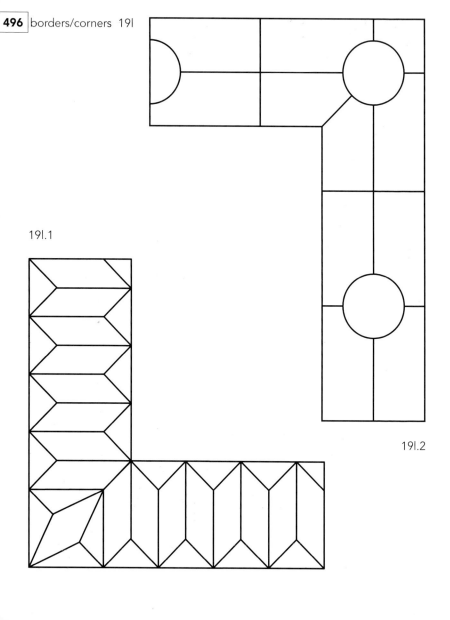

19l.1

19l.2

191.3

191.4

# 20.banners

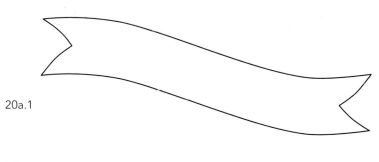

20a.1

20a.2

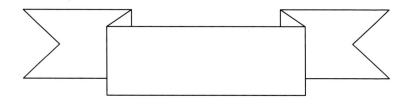

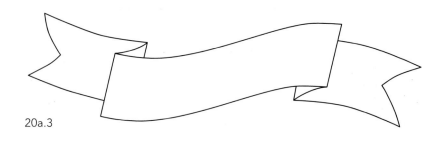

20a.3

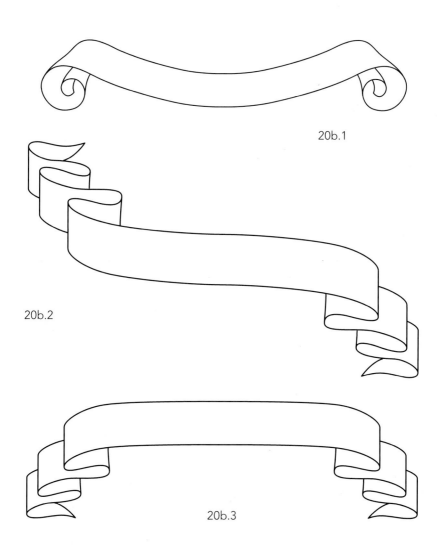

20b.1

20b.2

20b.3

20c.1

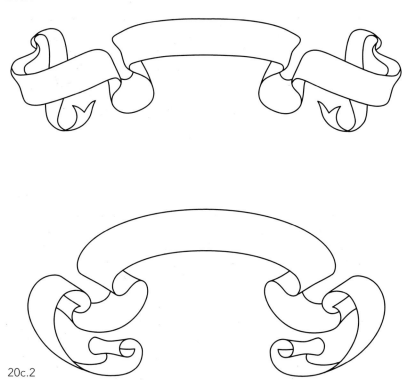

20c.2

20d.1

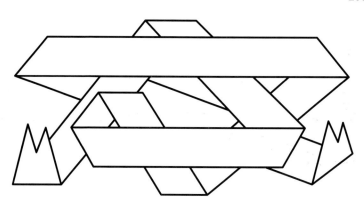

20d.2

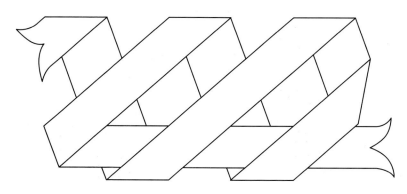

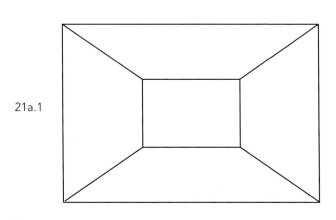

21a.1

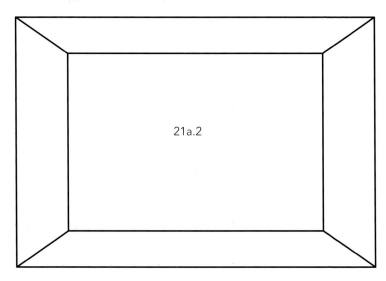

21a.2

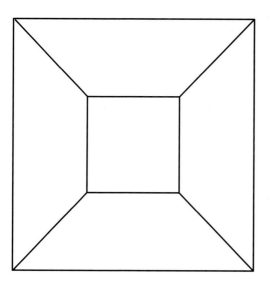

21b.1

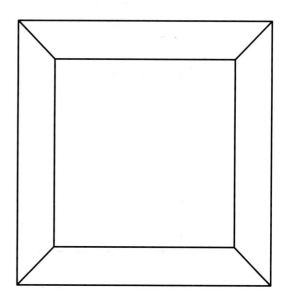

21b.2

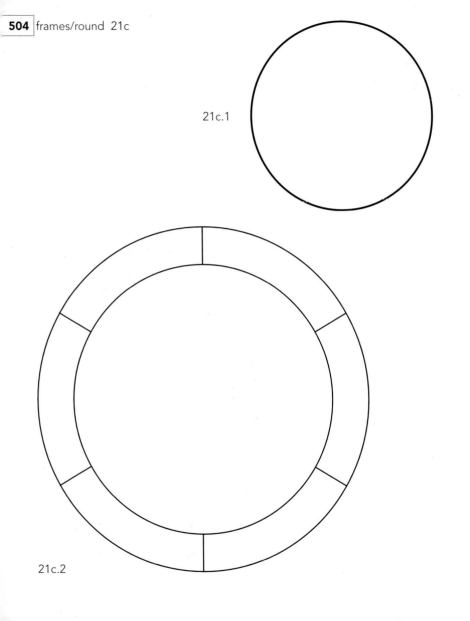

21c.1

21c.2

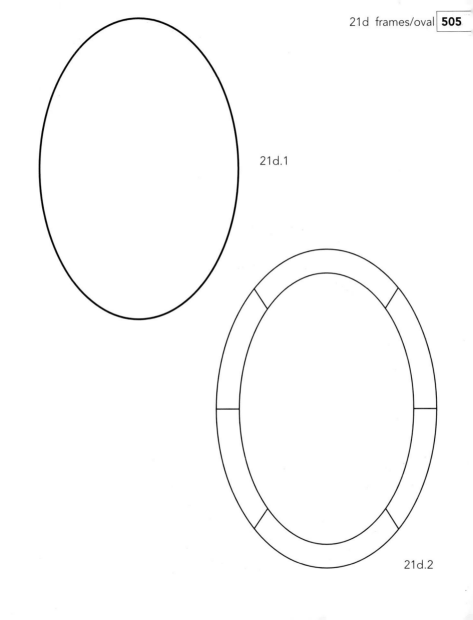

21d.1

21d.2

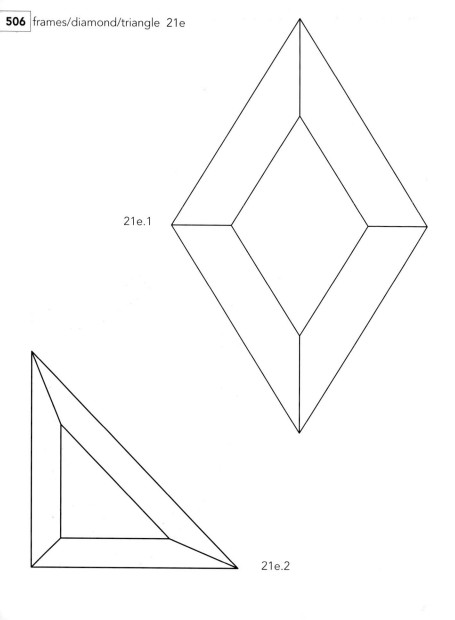

21e.1

21e.2

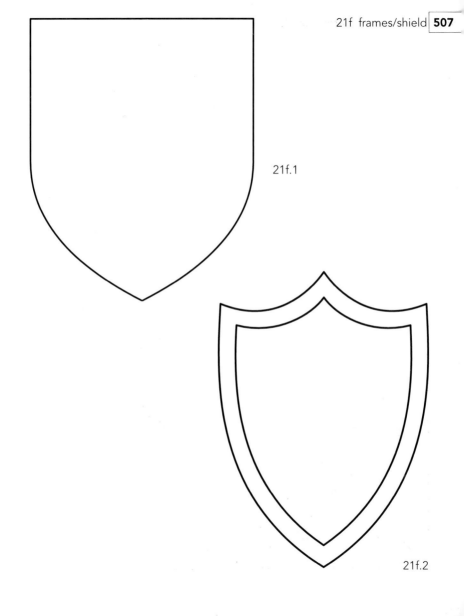

21f.1

21f.2

21g.1

21g.2

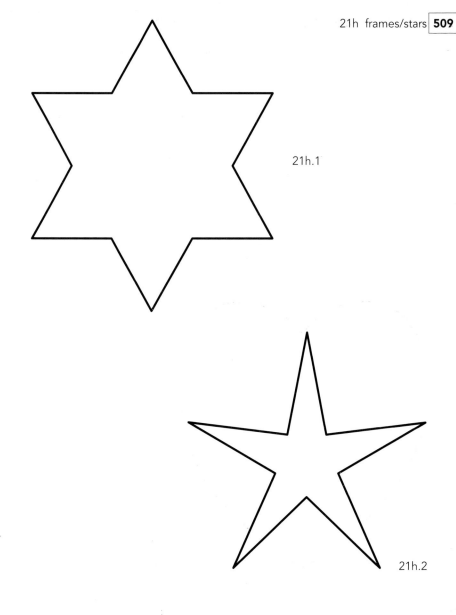

21h.1

21h.2

22.containers

22a.1

22a.2

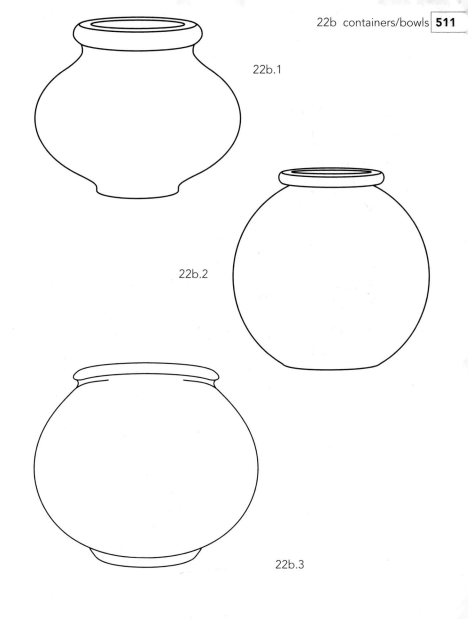

22b.1

22b.2

22b.3

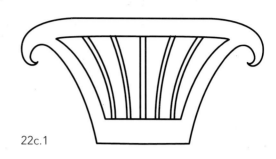

22c.1

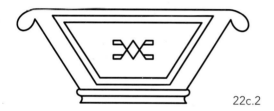

22c.2

22c.3

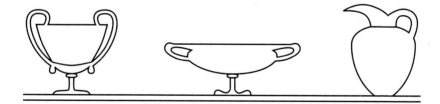

Some motifs in this book have previously appeared in *The Crafter's Pattern Source Book* by Mary McCarthy and *The Complete Guide to Glass Painting* by Alan D. Gear and Barry L. Freestone, both published by Collins & Brown. For more information about Rainbow Glass and its range of products, write to 85 Walkden Road, Worsley, Manchester M28 7BQ. Tel: 0161-790 3025.